Jews
IN WISCONSIN

Sheila Terman Cohen

WISCONSIN HISTORICAL SOCIETY PRESS

Published by the Wisconsin Historical Society Press
Publishers since 1855
The Wisconsin Historical Society helps people connect to the past
by collecting, preserving, and sharing stories. Founded in 1846,
the Society is one of the nation's finest historical institutions.

wisconsin history.org

Order books by phone toll free: (888) 999-1669
Order books online: shop.wisconsinhistory.org
Join the Wisconsin Historical Society: wisconsinhistory.org/membership

Publication of this book was made possible in part
by a generous gift from the Marcus Corporation.

Photographs identified with WHi or WHS are from the Society's collections;
address requests to reproduce these photos to the Visual Materials Archivist at the
Wisconsin Historical Society, 816 State Street, Madison, WI 53706.

Excerpts from Louis Heller's journals are reprinted with permission
from the Milwaukee Jewish Museum archives.

Printed in the United States of America
Designed by Jane Tenenbaum

20 19 18 17 16   1 2 3 4 5

Library of Congress Cataloging-in-Publication Data
Cohen, Sheila, 1939–, author.
Jews in Wisconsin / Sheila Terman Cohen. – First edition.
pages cm
ISBN 978-0-87020-744-0 (pbk. : alk. paper)–ISBN 978-0-87020-745-7 (ebook)
1. Jews–Wisconsin–History. I. Title.
F581.C64 2015
977.5'004924--dc23

2015035114

To my husband, Marc,
son of a Jewish Russian immigrant,
born and raised in Appleton, Wisconsin.
This is, in part, his story.

Nissan and Chai Sarah Alperovitz were among the early Jewish settlers who emigrated from Belarus to Sheboygan in the late 1800s to early 1900s. The Alperovitzes, pictured here in their Americanized clothing in 1937, arrived in 1906 along with other members of their family. Nissan became a cattle dealer and often served as cantor at the neighborhood synagogue, Ahavas Sholem Shul.

INTRODUCTION

Give me your tired, your poor, your huddled masses
yearning to breathe free,
the wretched refuse of your teeming shore.
Send these, the homeless, tempest-tost to me,
I lift my lamp beside the golden door!
—Emma Lazarus, Jewish poet

The famous lines of "The New Colossus," written by the Jewish poet Emma Lazarus in 1883 and engraved onto a bronze plaque at the base of the Statue of Liberty ten years later, symbolize America's historic openness to immigrants from all over the world. They could not have been more meaningful than they were to Jewish refugees who left their tempestuous pasts behind to find a safe haven in the United States.

Unlike other peoples who have come to the United States in search of a better life, the Jews who made that journey are united not by a single country of origin but by a shared history, one that spans four thousand years of varied experiences and locales. Over that long history, the word Jewish has at times been used to refer to a religion, a nationality, an ethnicity, and a culture. In a sense, all of these terms can be applied, depending on one's perspective.

Although there is no one credo that people must follow to call themselves Jewish, Judaism as a religion is guided by the Torah, the first five books of the Hebrew Bible. In its text, the Torah prescribes the basic tenets of the Jewish faith, which at its core rests on the belief in one God only. Extended from that concept are centuries of rabbinic interpretations that teach the principle that each individual is created in God's image and must therefore be treated with respect and justice. Such core ideas are underscored in the Hebrew words *tzedakah*, the importance of giving; *tshuvah*, the need to repent for one's wrongdoings; and *tefillah*, the need to pray and give thanks for one's blessings. The Ten Commandments found within the Torah reflect such ideals of honoring God and all of humanity.

Within the basic structure of the Jewish faith are three major divisions: Orthodox, Conservative, and Reform. Each reflects a different level of strict observance of Jewish religious practices, with Orthodox being the most observant, Conservative less so, and Reform the most liberal iteration of the same basic ideas. In more recent times, other groups have formed, including Reconstructionist and Humanist branches, which present their own nuanced beliefs and degree of observance. The Reconstructionist movement embraces a belief that God is present in all of nature and is not a single anthropomorphic entity, while the Humanist group focuses on the human capacity to create a better world without theistic underpinnings.

Although some people born into a Jewish home do not practice any form of the religion, their values often reflect the Jewish teachings of creating a just and equitable society. The Jewish tenet *tikkun olam*, translated from Hebrew as "repair of the world," is a call to Jews to do justice and pursue righteousness for all of humanity. Many Jews, whether religious or not, tend to manifest such concepts in their political and social values that aspire to create social justice for all.

However, Jews have frequently not been the beneficiary of the just and equitable society they espouse. Since their earliest origins in Mesopotamia nearly four thousand years ago, Jews have suffered periods of persecution that have driven them to find safe refuge elsewhere in the world. Throughout their earliest history, this monotheistic people found themselves at the mercy of Assyrian, Babylonian, Egyptian, and Roman rulers who persecuted them. As early as 1000 CE, large numbers of Jews fled these rulers and settled into what became the Germanic Confederation and Russian-dominated areas of Europe. Another stream of Jewish immigrants had put down roots in the areas that are now Spain, Portugal, Italy, Turkey, and North Africa. These diverse migrations to separate areas of the globe resulted in the formation of two distinct subcultures of Judaism referred to as Ashkenazim (German) and Sephardim (Spanish). Each group developed different religious traditions, dietary practices, and languages reflective of the area they occupied.

Throughout the ages, virulent myths about Judaism led to persecution of its followers. False tales of evil religious practices prevailed. The belief that Jews used the blood of Christian children in their rituals was passed down through generations. Jews were stigmatized as "Christ killers" by those who believed that non-Christians were inferior infidels.

Such beliefs led to violent attacks on Jewish communities and repeated attempts to force Jews to convert to Christianity. Resistance to forced conversion between the eleventh and thirteenth centuries gave way to the Roman Catholic Church's Crusades, a series of Holy Wars against non-Christians that brought about the wholesale slaughter of Muslims and Jews alike. In the late Middle Ages, a Roman Catholic tribunal conducted the Spanish Inquisition, forcing Jewish "heretics" (nonbelievers) to convert to Catholicism or be put to death. The interrogations led to the expulsion of all Jews from Spain in 1492. During the nineteenth and twentieth centuries, thousands of Jews living in czarist Russia were killed in three waves of pogroms (massacres). The most blatant and recent attempt to annihilate the Jewish people was the German Holocaust of World War II, during which six million Jews perished.

Each period of persecution made it necessary for the Jewish people to establish new beginnings all over the globe. From the mid-1800s to the 1900s, many of these Jewish immigrants made their way to the United States. Some ended up settling in Wisconsin. It is impossible to speak of a singular Jewish migration to Wisconsin. Each influx of Jewish settlers arrived at different periods in history via varied paths, with a range of varied life experiences. Over time, their diversity has blended into a rich mosaic of challenges and opportunities. Although relatively small in number, they have become an integral part of the strong and colorful fabric of immigrant cultures that make up the Wisconsin story.

JEWISH PIONEERS OF THE WILD WEST

The ultimate disinterest in new possibilities is death.
Life is an openness to stimulation.
—Rabbi Samuel Z. Glaser

In the early 1700s, long before Wisconsin became a state, it was part of the French-controlled Northwest Territory. Native American tribes who engaged in a flourishing fur trade inhabited most of the vast untamed wooded land where highly valued beaver pelts were hunted in abundance. With access to the Great Lakes and transport by boat, the Native Americans traded liberally with their Canadian neighbors to the north.

Throughout the 1700s, settlers from all over Europe and South America were beginning to inhabit the New World. They had traveled across the ocean to better their lot in a land that was reputed to hold the promise of treasure and the opportunity to exercise free will. Although a tiny fraction of the lot, about four thousand Jews were living in the eastern United States by 1830. The first to arrive were of Sephardic descent whose forefathers had been expelled from Spain in 1492. They sailed from the West Indies, Latin America, and Holland, places to which their ancestors had migrated in earlier times. A larger group of Ashkenazic Jews from various parts of Europe followed their Sephardic coreligionists to seek a good life in the colonies of the New World.

In spite of the fact that there were Jewish settlers on the East Coast as early as 1654, no Jew dared to openly move into the Northwest Territory under the dictates of the French Black Code of 1724. This edict banned Jews from living in any of the areas colonized by the French. In 1763, the French and Indian War ended, forcing the French to surrender the Northwest Territory and parts of Canada to the British. At that point a Jewish man or woman could at last legally settle into the western frontier that is now Wisconsin.

The first Jewish person known to do so was a young, ambitious man named Jacob Franks. Born in Britain, Franks moved to Quebec, Canada, with his parents in 1767. At age twenty-five, Franks traveled to Wisconsin in search of new opportunities and stimulation. A Jewish pioneer of sorts, Franks settled in what is now Green Bay, Wisconsin, in 1793. Despite his singularity, Franks quickly built good relationships with the Native American community. Eventually he entered into a common-law marriage with a Native American woman, who gave birth to five of his children. With mutual cooperation and the goodwill of the Native American fur traders, Franks built one of the most successful fur trading businesses in the area. As business soared, he recruited his nephew, John Lawe, from Canada to help him share the workload. Together they expanded their operation to DePere, Wisconsin, where they developed the first sawmill and gristmill to be built in the area in 1809. Although Franks eventually returned to Canada, Lawe remained. Most likely with political ambitions in mind, he converted from Judaism to Christianity. Lawe was appointed judge in Brown County and was later elected to the Wisconsin Territory legislature in 1836.

In the first two decades of the 1800s, only two other Jews were known to have lived in the Northwest Territory. One was Henry Joseph of Prairie du Chien, who converted to Catholicism under the guidance of Father Joseph Marie Drummon, a missionary who traveled through the area. Another Jewish inhabitant was an unnamed peddler. He reportedly was killed in Kaukauna by a Native American in 1820 in one of the many clashes between European settlers moving into the West and the tribes who already lived there.

In spite of these clashes, the early 1800s were by no means a stagnant period in the development of the region. As the fur trade continued in the northern portion of the Wisconsin Territory, lead mining became the dominant source of income for the southern part of the territory. By 1829, approximately four thousand miners toiled there to gather an abundant amount of the precious mineral that was particularly valued for its use in the manufacture of military ammunition. By the mid-1830s lead mining would prove to be the biggest boon to the area's economy. With the emergence of a lucrative industry, the floodgates opened to the "Yankees" (descendants of the first settlers) as well as the immigrant newcomers from the East. In the first half of the decade, more than two thousand travelers made the treacherous stagecoach journey westward over rocks and bumpy terrain. They settled in places including Mineral Point, Platteville, New Diggings, Shullsburg, and Belmont to find their fortunes. By the time the area became organized into the Wisconsin Territory in 1836, 50 percent of the nation's lead supply came from within its southwest boundaries.

No doubt, some Jewish pioneers were among the crowd that ventured west to set up shop or peddle their wares to the burgeoning population of lead miners. But it wasn't until the 1840s that the real surge of Jewish immigration to Wisconsin began to take place.

THE FIRST LARGE MIGRATION FROM
THE GERMAN CONFEDERATION

There are no problems, only opportunities for growth.
—Rebbetzin Denah Weinberg

As word spread throughout Europe of the New World and its vast opportunities, many people of the German Confederation were ready to leave their homeland for a better life. The Napoleonic War of 1812 had devastated much of the area, leaving farmland in short supply as the population grew ever larger.

With little fortune to leave behind and the promise of greater prosperity, German-speaking people of central Europe began a mass migration to the New World in the early 1840s, continuing to approximately 1880. During that time period, more than two hundred thousand Jews made their way to the United States as part of the larger wave of nearly five million immigrants from the German Confederation. Many of these still identified strongly with their Germanic homeland. Unlike future waves of Jewish immigrants, they had not been subjected to the severe persecution in their Germanic Confederate states of origin. Since the Enlightenment period of the 1700s, a philosophical trend toward reason and tolerance had helped overcome much of the anti-Semitism of earlier centuries. Although in many German states Jews continued to lack the economic rights of their peers and may not have been welcomed into the professional world of their Christian neighbors, by the nineteenth century Jews felt every bit as German as their fellow countrymen. Like other German immigrants from this period, their migration was more about opportunity than escape.

Large numbers of newcomers remained on the East Coast, but many were attracted to the area of Milwaukee, Wisconsin, which was quickly becoming one of the most desirable sites in the western territories. While later-arriving Jews dispersed throughout Wisconsin, the vast majority of these earliest immigrants made their homes in Milwaukee. Its location on Lake Michigan made it convenient for steamboats to transport goods to and from other ports, traveling via the Great Lakes and the Erie Canal, which opened in its entirety in 1825. Earlier settlers to the area had also made stagecoach travel easier by clearing fallen logs and removing large boulders from the dusty unpaved roads that led from east to west. And, most important to those hoping to begin a new life of opportunity, housing costs were less expensive in Milwaukee than in the cities on the bustling East Coast.

With its growing allure, former East Coast Yankees arrived in large numbers. German immigrants comprised the greatest share of the Milwaukee territory's growing population. Throughout the 1840s, the German language was more often spoken on the streets of Milwaukee than English, while German newspapers reported most of the news of the day.

In 1837, the Milwaukee area had been split into two major sections: Juneau Town on the east side of the Milwaukee River and Kilbourne Town on the west. The sides were named for the men who purchased the land, Solomon Juneau and Byron Kilbourne. Although the two areas merged into the city of Milwaukee by 1846, the division remained a significant demarcation in the city's cultural makeup. Most Germanic Jews eventually resided, practiced business, and worshipped on the east side. The area would become home to the wealthiest Jewish and Gentile residents alike. Meanwhile, eastern European Jews lived primarily on the city's west side with many other immigrants from such countries as Ireland, Poland, and Italy. Many of them would struggle to eke out a living for decades after their arrival.

The period between the late 1840s and into the 1850s saw a particularly large surge of German immigrants, due in part to the unsuccessful German Revolution of 1848. Known as the '48ers, German activists led uprisings in Vienna and Berlin, with the goal of forming a centralized, constitutional government. Facing exile after their defeat, many decided to try for a better life in the New World. Although few Jews took part in the uprising, many strongly aligned themselves with the '48ers' cause, joining them to leave their Germanic states to find a freer existence.

In a coincidence of history, 1848 was the same year that Wisconsin earned statehood. In an effort to attract people, the newly formed state placed advertisements in many European newspapers that read: "Come! In Wisconsin all men are free and equal before the law. . . . Religious freedom is absolute, and there is not the slightest connection between church and state." Many Germanic Jews and Gentiles heeded the call. By 1850, more than twenty thousand Germanic settlers had moved into Milwaukee, which had been dubbed the "cream city" because of its many buildings constructed of cream-colored brick. Of those, approximately 350 were German Jews, including members of seventy families, many of whom still identified strongly with their German heritage.

By the late 1850s, the number of Jewish families in Milwaukee stood at 2 percent of the population that numbered approximately forty-six thousand residents. A few Jewish men became part of the professional landscape. Nathan Pereles, a clerk from Prague, went from owning his own grocery store to becoming Milwaukee's first Jewish lawyer, and later a prominent banker. But most people initially gravitated to the type of work that had been available and familiar to them in the Old Country, where they had been self-reliant tradesmen and small-business owners. Once in the New World, some went into the sale of alcohol, tobacco, and groceries, while many others made livings as blacksmiths, locksmiths, shoemakers, and butchers. In time, with the shackles of Old World restrictions and prejudice set aside, many small-business owners rose to be heads of lucrative commercial concerns that they had built from the bottom up.

One such entrepreneur was Gabriel Shoyer. After arriving in his new homeland in 1844, he quickly established himself and sent for his five brothers. This common practice of sending for family members is referred to as chain migration. One of the brothers, Charles Shoyer, became Milwaukee's first Jewish physician, while the other brothers continued working in the needle trade that had been their occupation in the Old World. Shortly after arriving, Emanuel Shoyer opened a small tailor shop that eventually became one of the largest clothing stores in Milwaukee. By 1854 E. M. Shoyer and Co. employed seventy workers, including several of the Shoyer brothers, all of whom enjoyed the financial rewards of the successful venture.

While the Shoyers were building their business, David Adler arrived in New York from Bavaria in 1846 with ambitions to follow in their footsteps. Along with his extended family, Adler was soon to become a major competitor. Having sold his bakery in New York, he arrived in Milwaukee in 1852 with one thousand dollars cash in his pocket, as well as some East Coast business know-how. With improved industrial techniques, lower prices, and the skills of the Bavarian needle trade, Adler & Sons would become one of the largest clothing companies in the entire Midwest at the time. It grew to employ more than five hundred people, many of them fellow Jews from Germany.

The Friend family, headed first by brothers Henry and Elias Friend, added yet another competitor to the clothing manufacturing scene. Introducing the first steam-powered cutting machines in Milwaukee, their business soon rivaled the heights of Adler & Sons. By 1870, the manufacture and sale of clothing in Milwaukee was thriving, making it the city's third-largest industry in the mid-1800s.

The members of the Shoyer, Friend, and Adler families who made such large contributions to the clothing industry in Wisconsin would also become some of the most influential, generous, and active pillars of the Milwaukee Jewish community. They would be instrumental in shaping the early Reform religious movement in Wisconsin, developing the first Jewish temples, and establishing several important charitable organizations.

While the Germanic Jews were establishing themselves in Milwaukee, they saw a need for a communal place to share their faith. From their earliest arrival, a few would gather together in a home or a grocery store to worship on Yom Kippur, the day of atonement and the holiest day in the Jewish religion. By 1848, Emanuel Shoyer purchased land for a Jewish cemetery, and by 1850 the first congregation, Congregation Emanu-El (God is with us) was formed, led by Solomon Adler as its president.

True to an old bit of Jewish humor, "If three Jews are marooned on an island, there will soon be three synagogues." Such was the case with Milwaukee's Germanic Jews. By 1856, Emanu-El B'ne Jeshurun Congregation was established, as a merger between Ahavath Emunah (1854) and Anshe Emeth (1855). Although it was the largest congregation in the city, it was soon followed by several others, each with slight differences of religious tradition and practice that were carried from the congregants' particular region of origin.

The German Jewish population's predominant religious preference was Reformed Judaism. Unlike the Orthodox Jews of Eastern Europe who strictly practiced kosher dietary laws and distinguished themselves in other ways from their Christian neighbors, German Jews had assimilated in many ways into their Germanic society, including dropping their supposedly old-fashioned Orthodox practices.

Not all found community solely in the arms of religious congregations, however. For those who associated with the likes of the freethinking '48ers, political movements and Jewish organizations accommodated their secular needs. Among them, many Jewish charities were established in Milwaukee during the 1860s and '70s. One of the largest was the B'nai B'rith fraternal organization, which bore the credo "Benevolence, Brotherly Love, and Humanity." With those high ideals in mind, the men's social group took on a project of establishing housing for the more than five hundred orphaned Jewish and Gentile children of Milwaukee. Although most German Jewish families were able to financially take care of themselves in the mid-1800s, one of the most important Jewish commandments, *tzedakah* (Hebrew word meaning righteousness or justice and commonly used to refer to acts of giving), dictated that they provide aid to those in need.

Although their German identification remained strong, Milwaukee's Jews also made efforts to assimilate into the American way of life. Members of the Congregation Emanu-El regularly celebrated Thanksgiving and other distinctly American holidays. Jews also often commingled with Gentiles in the German society of Milwaukee, joined German fraternal organizations, and enrolled their children in the German-English Academy. Leaders in the German Gentile community enthusiastically attended Jewish events at which they were frequently asked to speak.

A MOVEMENT INTO
WISCONSIN'S SMALL TOWNS

It has been my privilege then to have been
a human being on the planet Earth;
and to have been an American, a writer, a Jew.
—Edna Ferber in *My Peculiar Treasure*

Although Milwaukee remained the hub for 80 percent of Wisconsin's Jewish population throughout the nineteenth century, a trickling of mostly German Jews had begun to move out of the city and into the state's smaller rural areas in the mid-1800s. By 1851, railroad tracks had become part of Wisconsin's landscape, making Milwaukee's access to Lake Michigan and steamboat travel less vital. Roads were in better shape, having been cleared of boulders and trees by earlier settlers. In addition, some business owners sensed that better opportunities and less competition might be found in smaller cities such as Madison, Stevens

Point, La Crosse, Appleton, Wausau, Superior, Green Bay, Sheboygan, Beloit, Racine, and Hurley.

La Crosse welcomed its first Jewish resident, John M. Levy, in 1845 when the area was still known as Prairie La Crosse. Levy, of British descent, became a fur trader in the area. As a respected civic leader, he not only befriended immigrant newcomers to the city, but also was eager to build bridges between the Jewish settlers and the rest of the community. He did so by inviting his Christian neighbors to his home for religious services that included every denomination. Having gained the deep respect of the people of La Crosse, he served as mayor of the city for three terms in the 1850s.

With a predisposition to becoming involved with matters of social justice, both German Jews and Russian co-religionists that followed took an interest in local politics and frequently ran for elected positions. Many prominent leaders won the confidence and respect of their community and were elected to fill state and local offices. John Levy of La Crosse, Alexander Billstein of Neenah, Edward Poznanski of Chippewa Falls, Michael Newald of Ft. Howard, and Joseph Mann of Two Rivers all served as mayor as their respective cities in the 1800s. Baruch Schleisinger Weil, founder of Schleisingerville (now Slinger), served as state senator from 1852 to 1880, and Leon Silverman of Mequon was state senator in the 1850s. David Hammel was state representative from 1876 to 1877 and was elected mayor of Appleton in the early 1900s.

According to the official census, a store clerk by the name of Aaron Boscowitz was the first Jewish resident of Madison in 1850. However, it was Samuel Klauber who led the way for many others who followed. After leaving the Germanic area of Bohemia in 1847, Klauber peddled fabrics, threads, and other products in New York for a year before finding a job in the dry goods business in Lake Mills, Wisconsin. By 1851 he had worked his way to Madison. Despite the fact that much of the area was ensconced in vast groves of forests, word had gotten out that the growing city of 1,525 people could use a clothing store. After walking the gas-lit wooden sidewalks, periodically joined by wandering chickens and pigs, Klauber selected a location in which to invest his three hundred dollars in savings. That spot turned out to be a sixteen-by-forty-foot frame structure where he set up shop. However, starting his business wasn't easy. The railroad track would not stretch that far west for another six years. It took two weeks for a letter to reach New York, where many of the clothes were manufactured. Despite such obstacles, the small undertaking eventually changed location and became a successful clothing and dry goods business. Between 1851 and 1860, twenty Jewish families followed Klauber's example, traveling west to settle in Madison. Nathan Moody, the first Jewish dentist in town, was among them.

Just as Samuel Klauber led the way to Madison, so too did he take on several important leadership roles in his adopted home. Like so many other Jewish settlers in Wisconsin, Klauber was concerned with matters both religious and secular. Among his many civic activities, he became a member and curator of the Wisconsin Historical Society, where his portrait was hung with the words "Pioneer merchant of Madison" written at its base.

In rural and urban areas alike, devoted Jews initially squeezed into someone's home for religious services. It was important to have a *minyan* (a group of at least ten men to recite ritual prayers). In 1856, Klauber established Madison's first Reform congregation. A congregation of seventeen Jewish immigrant families gathered at his home. The group eventually purchased land for temple Ahavath Achim (Brother Love), where Klauber became president. The small Madison sandstone building, which originally stood at 214 West Washington Avenue, was later named Shaare Shomaim (Gates of Heaven). It was moved to the city's James Madison Park in 1971 for historical preservation. Although it is used for a variety of secular activities, the building continues to open its doors for Jewish religious services on the holiest days of the Jewish calendar, Rosh Hashanah (the new year) and Yom Kippur (the day of atonement).

Despite the growth of Madison's Jewish population in later years, Appleton claimed the second-largest number of Jewish residents in the late 1800s. Two of the most famous Jews from Wisconsin made their home there. Eric Harry Weiss emigrated with his parents from Budapest, Hungary, to Appleton in 1883 at the age of nine. His father, Mayer Weiss, had been hired to be the city's first rabbi. Unfortunately, Rabbi Weiss could deliver his sermons only in broken English or his native Hungarian language, which proved to be unacceptable to the new congregants of the Temple Zion Reform Jewish congregation. Although Rabbi Weiss failed to keep his job, his son, who later changed his name to Harry Houdini, went on to become an enormous success in an entirely different field. "The Great Houdini" entertained and beguiled audiences throughout the world with his feats of magic and escape.

Edna Ferber was another famous name that helped to put Appleton on the map. Born to a Jewish Hungarian storekeeper, she and her family arrived in Appleton in 1897 when she was twelve years old. After she attended high school and then, briefly, Lawrence College in Appleton, her writing talents were soon realized and developed as a journalist for the *Appleton Post Crescent*. Later, her notable novels *Giant, Showboat,* and the 1924 Pulitzer Prize–winning *So Big* brought her praise throughout the literary world. Her 1938 book *A Peculiar Treasure* details her memories of growing up in Appleton. Ferber concluded her book with an expression of gratitude for the life she had led in small-town Wisconsin.

As the transition across the state progressed, Appleton's Jewish population grew to 143 residents. It was followed by La Crosse with 106 and Madison with 76 inhabitants who identified themselves as Jewish in 1877. Stevens Point also became home to a growing number of Jewish settlers as the next wave of Jewish Eastern European settlers followed in the footsteps of their German predecessors. As Jewish residents moved into Stevens Point, beginning with German immigrant Isaac Brill in 1869, the population grew steadily until the mid-1900s.

NATIONAL TROUBLES MOUNT

God is present whenever a peace treaty is signed.
—Rabbi Nachman Ben Simha

Although the Jews and Gentiles of Wisconsin's small towns seemed to work quite well together in the mid-1800s, the Southern and Northern halves of the country demonstrated far less harmony. The Southern states, which relied heavily on slave labor to maintain their agrarian economy, strongly opposed the abolitionists' plan to outlaw slavery in newly established territories and threatened to secede from the United States. In response, President Abraham Lincoln declared war in 1861 in an effort to preserve the union.

Nearly ten thousand Jewish soldiers fought alongside their fellow countrymen in the Civil War. Many of the state's Jewish men served in the Union's Twenty-Fourth and Twenty-Sixth Wisconsin infantries, both of which endured some of the most difficult battles, including the Battle of Gettysburg. Like their Gentile counterparts, many Jewish soldiers were badly wounded or died in combat.

Several survivors distinguished themselves for their bravery and courage. Although his Jewish roots are a point of controversy, some historians have considered Frederick Salomon of Manitowoc to be one of Wisconsin's most notable Jewish Civil War heroes. Salomon, who recorded his religion as Jewish, rose to the rank of major general. His three brothers, Charles, Edward, and Herman, also served valiantly in the war, while Edward gained further prominence as the eighth governor of Wisconsin in 1861. Although Frederick claimed to be of Jewish heritage, each of his brothers professed to Christian denominations, thus leaving the family ancestry in question. All of the Salomon brothers are honored for their patriotic duty with a monument that was erected in front of the courthouse in Manitowoc.

While not all Jewish men of the state served in the war, some helped in ways that were unsung, though very valuable. In Milwaukee, Adler & Sons manufactured a large bulk of the Union's blue uniforms. In Madison, Samuel Klauber and his wife, Caroline, led the way to raise money for families that had sacrificed their breadwinners to the war effort.

Although an estimated 6,300 US Jews served in the Union army and more than 3,000 fought on the Confederate side, many of these soldiers faced anti-Semitism in exchange for their service. In the South, Jewish soldiers who died in battle could not be buried in the official Confederate cemetery. Instead, they were buried separately at the Jewish Confederate cemetery in Richmond, Virginia, thought to be one of the only Jewish military burial grounds in the country. Examples of wartime anti-Semitism also could be found in the North, where an order by Union general Ulysses S. Grant illustrated that some Americans still viewed Jews as strangers who could not be trusted. To weed out traders thought to be illegally dealing in Southern cotton on the Union side, Grant accused Jews as a whole of being responsible and ordered them out of any area he commanded. "Post commanders will see that all of this class of people be furnished passes and required to leave, and any one returning after such notification will be arrested and held in confinement until an opportunity occurs of sending them out as prisoners," Grant's order read. In return, President Lincoln replied, "I do not like to hear a class or nationality condemned on account of a few sinners." On January 4, 1863, the order was rescinded.

While some Jews may have faced anti-Semitism in the military, Milwaukee's Jewish population was welcomed to participate in the political and cultural affairs of the city in the years following the war. As they did so, there is no doubt that they greatly contributed to the city's progress. One strong testimonial to this fact appeared in a July 20, 1872, editorial in the *Milwaukee Daily Sentinel*:

> The Israelites of Milwaukee are numbered among our most respected and progressive citizens, and not without cause. Not a business enterprise, scheme for the amelioration of mankind, or movement for the social advancement of our people is without their support and influence. The city is in fact largely indebted to them for the proud position she holds today.

A LARGER RUSSIAN MIGRATION

The most ignorant immigrant on landing,
proceeds to give and receive greeting, to eat, see,
and rise after the manner of his own country;
wherein he is corrected, admonished, and laughed at,
whether by interested friends or the most indifferent
strangers; and his American experience is thus begun.
—Mary Antin, Jewish immigrant from Russia
and author of *The Promised Land*, 1906

Although the pace of immigration had slowed significantly during the Civil War, it wasn't long before another surge of Jewish immigrants arrived in the United States. With anti-Semitism boiling over in their homelands, Jews from Russia and other Russian-dominated countries began to travel en masse to points on the East Coast. However, lack of jobs and overcrowding made it impossible for all of them to settle there. In time, many would make their way west to Wisconsin, changing the face of the Jewish immigrant life in the state from that time forward.

For centuries, slanderous tales about Jews fueled a burning anti-Jewish sentiment among Russians. Some Russians clung to the belief that Jews were "Christ killers" who drained the blood of Christian children for their religious rituals. Under the reign of the Romanov dynasty, Russian Jews became pawns in the hands of the czarist rulers. In rollercoaster fashion, the restrictions on them tightened and eased, depending on the whims of the particular czar in power. In 1791 Catherine the Great created the Pale of Settlement, an area of land that included part of Poland, which was acquired by Russia in the eighteenth century. Jewish families were forced to live there in impoverished shtetls (communal villages). This confinement bred laws that prohibited Jews from trading outside of the Pale, restricted them from entering universities, and kept them from pursuing professions.

Czar Nicholas I (1825–1855) delivered some of the harshest decrees to befall the Jewish population. Under the guise of conscription into the Russian military, he ordered Jewish boys to be taken from their homes at age thirteen. Often the boys were forced to be baptized into the Russian Orthodox Church and punished if they refused.

Under the more liberal-minded Alexander II, some Jews joined the activist movement the People's Will, which advocated social, economic, and political reforms for Russians outside the aristocracy. Although comparatively small in number, activist Jews were blamed for Alexander II's assassination in 1881. His successor son, Alexander III, ordered brutal attacks (pogroms) on Jews in the Pale of Settlement. Such attacks resulted in the pillage, rape, and massacre of thousands of Jews throughout the next decade and into the 1900s.

The May Laws of 1882 stripped away any rights that Jewish survivors might have previously gained during brief periods of relaxed restrictions. Some fled by foot to a more enlightened western Europe. Most dispersed to South Africa, England, Palestine and the United States with the help of the host country that agreed to take them in. Two million eastern European Jews made their way to America during that period.

In desperation, they piled on to steerage vessels in filthy, packed conditions that often led to illness. Infectious respiratory diseases and dysentery quickly spread among the passengers. Nevertheless, they clung to a collective hope that life would be better in America. At least they would be safe from slaughter and their children would know a freedom that they had never experienced.

Upon the immigrants' arrival at Ellis Island, overworked clerks quickly pushed each person through long lines to check documentation.

In many instances, new refugees left the line realizing that, not only had they left their homeland behind, but their identity had been changed as they assumed new names. Shimon Kitigordsky left Kiev, Russia, in 1910 to avoid conscription into the Russian military. His future wife, Hashke Kropchon, fled the country to escape the pernicious pogroms. They began their lives in Milwaukee as Sam Gross and Hilda Levine. Whether they chose to change their distinctly Russian names or had them changed upon entrance into the United States, their daughter, Ann Meadows, later told a Richland Center interviewer, "We, the second generation, are living with borrowed names."

The first word that Russian immigrants were to arrive in Milwaukee came without much advance warning. With no more than a telegram from Canadian immigration officials, a trainload of 218 Russian refugees made their way on June 27, 1882, from their first point of dispersion in Montreal, Canada, to a city that was unprepared to welcome them.

Although the newly arrived Russians were of the same Ashkenazi ancestry as the 2,500 German Jews already residing in Milwaukee, the similarity seemed to stop there. Because they had led an entirely different existence in the shtetls of the Russian Empire than the assimilated Jews of Germany, they appeared to be worlds apart. The newcomers arrived in drab and shabby clothing, a testimony to their impoverished condition in the Old World. The men, bearing long, unkempt beards, came steeped in the study of Talmud (rabbinic interpretations of the Bible). But no matter how literate in Yiddish, their mother tongue, no man, woman, or child living in the isolated shtetls had been privy to a secular education, as their German predecessors had been. In addition, their Orthodox religious ways made it hard to imagine that they shared a common bond with their German Jewish counterparts who embraced the Reform movement of Judaism.

The vast differences created a conflict for the bulk of the Wisconsin German Jews who had long since eased their way into the American way of life. In accordance with a basic tenet of Judaism, *tzedakah*, they were compelled to offer help to those in need. At the same time, they feared that their close association with the new arrivals would set them apart from the society that had welcomed them as full participants.

Rae Rushe was one such immigrant from Germany whose family had comfortably settled in Milwaukee when she was a child. By the time Rushe was an assimilated young woman, she had fallen in love with and married a Jewish man who at age eleven had escaped the Polish portion of the Pale of Settlement. Their daughter, Ruth, born of the German–Eastern European union, later recounted in a 1962 interview, "My [German maternal] grandmother regarded me as a mongrel, tainted with mixed blood."

FULFILLING THE BASIC TEACHINGS
OF THE TORAH

Tzedakah is not about giving; tzedakah is about being.
—Rabbi Bradley Shavit Artson

Despite the chasm between the settled German Jewish residents in Milwaukee and the eastern European immigrants, it was clear that something had to be done to help the new arrivals, who needed food, shelter, clothing, and all the basic necessities of daily life. In accordance with *tzedakah*, one of Milwaukee's most respected Jewish leaders, David Adler, led the way in establishing the Russian Relief Association. Realizing the daunting task ahead, he decided to approach the city's mayor, John Stowell, for help. In turn, on June 29, 1882, the mayor issued a plea to the city at large, stating, "These people have been driven from a despotic government by the most cruel autocracies known in the history of man. They are in God's image and entitled to room and life on God's earth. We must temporarily afford them sustenance and shelter until they can help themselves."

It soon became evident that the 218 arrivals in Milwaukee were only the beginning of what was to become a flood of eastern European refugees from the late 1880s and into the 1900s, as the devastating pogroms continued. The Milwaukee German Jews soon realized that more had to be done. As an emergency tactic, the disheveled groups of refugees were housed in abandoned factories where empty industrial vats were used as bathtubs. Gradually, families began to settle into the Haymarket area, one of the most rundown regions of the city west of the Milwaukee River. There they lived in old dilapidated apartment houses that often didn't have running water or heat.

In response to the slum conditions that the eastern European Jews lived in, both men and women in the German Jewish community quickly organized a series of charities to help reduce the pain of resettlement. The Hebrew Relief Fund was set up to provide fuel and food. The Widow and Orphan Society specifically helped women and children who arrived without a male breadwinner. The members of the Ladies Relief Sewing Society busied themselves making clothing, shoes, and bedding. And the Sisterhood of Personal Service set out to improve the physical condition of the poor. These individual groups and others later melded into United Hebrew Charities, then Federated Jewish Charities, and eventually became known as the Milwaukee Jewish Federation.

Once the bare necessities of the refugees were beginning to be met, the charitable spotlight focused on culturally uplifting them through education—thought to be the best ticket out of poverty. In 1891 the Jewish Alliance School began to enroll one hundred students free of charge. The immigrant settlers learned to replace their Yiddish language with English while studying American civics, politics, and history.

Seeing the wisdom in the education movement, a prominent woman of the Milwaukee German Jewish community, Elizabeth (Lizzie) Black Kander, stepped forward to begin the Milwaukee Jewish Mission in 1886. Boys and girls were taught useful crafts and physical activities with the goal of instilling perseverance and American patriotism. Each class day ended with the singing of patriotic songs, such as "America: My Country Tis of Thee," which was written in 1831 and served as the country's national anthem into the 1900s.

Four years later, Lizzie Kander expanded her vision by opening the Settlement, a forerunner of the Jewish Community Center. The Settlement was a place where kids could come to join literary clubs, visit a public library, and engage in athletic activities. Adult night classes were soon added. Since 70 percent of the residents of 1900 Milwaukee were born outside of the country, the Settlement opened its doors to Jewish and non-Jewish immigrants alike. It was a place to find out about the American way of life, and even take a hot bath or shower.

Chances are many kitchens still have an old copy of *The Settlement Cookbook*, handed down from one generation to the next. Kander compiled the assortment of recipes in 1891 to raise funds for the Settlement. Selling for fifty cents, it managed to garner five hundred dollars in profit in the first year. It went on to sell 1.5 million copies in more than forty printings over the next century, distributed around the globe.

While Lizzie Kander was helping to assimilate newcomers, others worked to fill another great void in the city. Healthcare was either non-existent or too expensive for most immigrants, who arrived with little more than the clothes on their backs. Because of the cramped living quarters, diseases were easily transmitted in the ramshackle immigrant neighborhoods. Cases of smallpox, typhoid, malaria, and waterborne cholera were common, frequently killing children by the age of five.

In the early 1900s the Federated Jewish Charities established the first hospital in the Haymarket area, housed in an empty YWCA building leased by Jewish businessman Max Landauer. When the building proved too small to serve the needs of the burgeoning population, it was re-placed by Mt. Sinai Hospital, a fifteen-bed facility in a strongly German area on the east side. Like the Settlement, it opened its doors to all ethnic groups and more often than not did not charge for services rendered to the poor.

After several expansions, it became clear that the people who flocked to Mt. Sinai with a variety of illnesses needed a larger place to receive treatment. Once again, with the help of Max Landauer and other philanthropists, a new four-story, one-hundred-bed state-of-the-art Mt. Sinai hospital became a reality on November 15, 1914. It would become known as the best hospital in southeast Wisconsin and continued to charge nothing for those who couldn't afford to pay.

THE ARPIN EXPERIMENT

The status quo proves the most illusory of goals.
—David Reisman, sociologist

Like Milwaukee, other large cities around the country were also strug-gling to house burgeoning immigrant populations. Although there had been an earlier movement of German Jews into small communities, the gradual exodus of Jewish immigrants did not take place fast enough to solve the overcrowded conditions in the larger cities. To facilitate the movement, the Jewish Agriculture Society established the Industrial Removal Office in New York in 1901 with the mission of finding jobs for refugees by dispersing them across the country. Under its administration,

3,700 Jewish residents were resettled in seventy-four Wisconsin towns and cities.

Adolf Rich, a successful Milwaukee businessman, was one of the early advocates for the Industrial Removal Office's mission. In 1904, the one-time farmer came up with a plan that had not been tried before. He purchased 720 acres in the rural area of Arpin, Wisconsin, with the idea of recruiting eastern European families to establish a community and farm the land. They would be given forty acres, two horses, one cow, five dollars per week, and a small wooden dwelling. Initially, five Jewish families were willing to be part of the experiment, which included a two-day train trip from Milwaukee to Arpin and a campaign to get many others to follow. Eventually, thirteen additional kindred spirits brought their children and a few possessions to begin a farming existence.

In a 1976 interview for the *Milwaukee Journal*, Max Leopold, a former Arpin resident who had arrived at age fourteen, recalled, "We were eighteen Jewish families without a farmer in our midst. Most of us had apprenticed as tradesman in the Old Country." Despite the lack of preparation, the Jewish settlers in Arpin cleared the land, learned to work the soil, and built log homes. They even established a synagogue in 1915. What no one had counted on, however, was that the Yiddish-speaking residents of Arpin began to feel isolated from their cultural roots. In time, all of them left their farms and headed back to Milwaukee or followed the diaspora trend to smaller cities in Wisconsin that had begun to develop.

THE GREAT DIVIDE

You'll never find a better sparring partner than adversity.
—Golda Meir

For those who either remained in or returned to Milwaukee, a great abyss still existed between the German Jews and the eastern European arrivals in the early 1900s. Most of the forerunners from the Germanic regions were comfortably settled into nice homes on the east side of Milwaukee, while the eastern Europeans remained clustered in the overcrowded slums of Haymarket housing, with their cracked walls, filthy hallways, and putrid odors.

Not only did socioeconomic factors contribute to the chasm, but so too did political and religious points of view. The Russian immigrants, who had been constantly exposed to the brutality of the czarist rulers, brought with them a collective Zionist mentality. As Zionists, their hope was that Jews would one day have their own homeland, where they could once and for all shed their fears of life-threatening persecution. Such insecurities were viewed as unpatriotic by the established German Jews, who could not yet imagine the atrocities their Russian counterparts had experienced, or the rising anti-Semitism faced by their former countrymen who had remained in Germany.

The birth of Germany as a nation in 1871 engendered a sense of nationalism that fueled a growing belief in Aryan superiority. Various theorists in the mid-1800s publically espoused scathing anti-Semitic feelings. The great composer Richard Wagner joined their ranks by writing, "I hold the Jewish race to be the born enemy of pure humanity and everything noble in it." Expressing the views of a growing number of Germans, Wagner demanded in his writings that the Jews, who comprised 1 percent of the population, get out of the country. Although the changing mood captured the attention of Jews in Europe, many of the German Jews living in Wisconsin regarded the signs of trouble as a temporary situation.

Two decades later, Alfred Dreyfus, the first Jewish officer in the French army, was accused of selling military secrets to the Germans. Despite the fact that the information he was accused of sending was not in his handwriting, he was tried in a biased courtroom, stripped of his medals in a humiliating public display, and condemned to life in prison in 1894. Although the lack of supportive evidence in the case made it apparent that the charges against the thirty-five-year-old officer had been trumped up, the accusation stirred an underlying anti-Jewish sentiment, as chants of "Kill the Jews, kill the Jews!" were shouted in the streets of Paris.

For many Jews, such events began to foreshadow the need for a safe Jewish homeland. Under the leadership of Theodore Herzl, a European journalist who had been keeping his eye on the fomenting anti-Semitic atmosphere, the first Zionist Congress was held in Basel, Switzerland. It was a gathering of Jewish leaders who believed in the formation of a Jewish homeland. The German Jews in Milwaukee were still leery of aligning themselves with such a movement. They continued to believe that the new anti-Semitism in their country of origin was confined to a fringe group and would simply fade away.

In stark contrast to the German attitude, many eastern European Jews in Milwaukee believed strongly in Zionism. They banded together to form a branch of the Knights of Zion organization in 1899. The group eventually turned Milwaukee into a Midwestern hub of Zionist activity, attracting five hundred people to its convention in 1910.

In 1907, those eastern European immigrants with a Socialist bent formed a Milwaukee branch of the national organization Arbeiter Ring (Workmen's Circle). It embraced secular Judaism and an anti-assimilation philosophy that included keeping the Yiddish language alive. Unlike the Knights of Zion, members dispensed with thoughts of a Jewish homeland and focused on goals of providing benefits and better conditions for the wage earners of Milwaukee. The organization soon would branch out to other Wisconsin cities, including Madison, Eau Claire, and Sheboygan, where it established after-school programs, theater groups, and summer camps that espoused their philosophies and exposed their members' children to their native tongue. Sylvia Grunes, a Madison resident who attended Arbeiter Ring activities, remembers, "The Talmud Torah kids [those who attended religious school] called us Communists." But despite the derogatory reference, Grunes said she has wonderful memories of the plays she performed in and the camps she attended in her youth.

Many Russian immigrants arrived in the United States shortly before the curtain rose on the Bolshevik Revolution of 1917, which overthrew the czarist regime. Along with their few personal items, some carried with them the activist verve and socialist ideals of the pre-revolution period. Those who settled in Milwaukee could not have picked a better place to give vent to their socialist leanings. Victor Berger, a secular Jew who had arrived from Austria–Hungary in 1898, led the Socialist movement that grew into a strong force within Milwaukee's political milieu of the time. No other city in the country would elect as many representatives and mayors who declared themselves card-carrying Socialists.

Although eastern European immigrants were grateful to find a safe haven in their new homeland, their collective social conscience led them to point out injustices where they saw them. The industrial factories, rife with exploitation of their workers, were realistic targets. Men, women, and children worked sixteen hours a day, six days a week for very little pay. Housing, which was sometimes attached to the factory, might be a one-room flat for a family, often with no running water or electricity. In an effort to combat such abhorrent conditions, the Socialist movement aligned itself with Milwaukee's emerging labor unions, joining their voices to causes that helped abolish child labor and fight for better pay, shorter hours, and safer working conditions.

While the German Jews on the east side of the river tried their best not to make waves in their new home, the eastern European Jews of Haymarket and beyond remained active in the Knights of Zion, the Arbeiter Ring, and a third group, the Po'alei Zion, which combined the ideologies of both protecting labor and establishing a Jewish homeland.

One of the most famous and outspoken of the eastern European Jewish immigrants to join the activist movement was Goldie Mabowehz, a young woman who arrived in Milwaukee from Pinsk (part of modern-day Belarus) in 1906 at the age of eight. She later recounted that she had been overwhelmed to find herself in a modern city with such luxuries as soda pop, ice cream cones, and the five-story Schuster's Department Store, where her father took her shopping for an "Americanized" wardrobe. The wide-eyed child from Belarus would later become Golda Meir, the first woman prime minister of Israel.

Peter Ottenstein, who arrived in the United States in 1905, was a friend of Goldie Mabowehz's and an active member of the Milwaukee Labor Zionist movement. At the age of seventy-one, he recalled the days when dreaming of a Jewish homeland was not regarded kindly by most German Jews in the city. "They called us traitors," he remembered. "When Golda heard that they called us traitors, she cried. And I said, 'Golda, now if you can cry, you're eligible to join the labor movement, our Zionist movement.' And then she joined."

While numerous Orthodox synagogues sprung up in the Haymarket area, depending on the congregants' region of origin, the Jews on the east side of the river continued to practice a Reform brand of Judaism. Men and women sat together rather than being separated by a *mechitza* (screened barrier) during religious services. English often replaced the Hebrew prayers that were chanted in the Orthodox synagogues. Kosher dietary practices also were dispensed with, making dishes of pork and shellfish perfectly acceptable on many east side dinner tables.

EAST MEETS WEST IN THE WATERSHED MOMENTS OF WORLD WAR I

*When we are no longer able to change a situation,
we are challenged to change ourselves.*
—Viktor Franki, *Man in Search of Meaning*

The twentieth century brought about two world wars that altered Jewish life in Wisconsin and around the world forever. Until World War I began, neither Russian nor German Jewish immigrants living in the United States had been pressed to declare their loyalty to their new homeland. In 1914, when Germany and its allied Central Powers joined in battle against Britain, France, and Russia, great conflict and unease arose in the hearts and minds of the Jewish newcomers.

German Jews, although assimilated to American customs and way of life, continued to hold on to a romantic notion of their birthplace. Some sent their children back to Germany to be educated, and many continued to speak the German language and read German newspapers. With strong emotional ties, many felt compelled to support their homeland in time of war. Victor Berger, an Austrian-Hungarian Jew who arrived in Milwaukee in 1881 and was elected to a term in the US House of Representatives on the Socialist ticket, led a group of antiwar protestors in Wisconsin.

Many Russian Jews also found themselves temporarily feeling ambivalent about their allegiances, but for different reasons. The allied forces included Russia, a country that had brutalized them in the recent past, and continued to overrun the shtetls in which their families and friends remained. During the war, reports coming to America confirmed that thousands of Jews in Russia were being pushed eastward. The harsh winter took the lives of countless refugees as they sought shelter and food. With word of such misery, the Russian Jews of Milwaukee felt compelled to help their former countrymen. Chaired by Milwaukee's Rabbi Solomon Scheinfeld, the eastern European Jews established the Ezra Betzar (help in distress) war relief fund on behalf of the "war sufferers" in Russia. Using the slogan "A Life Blessed for a Life Blighted," they tirelessly approached Jewish as well as Gentile communities. Many donated what they could, with a common goal of sending aid to the Russian Jews who were suffering half a world away.

Although the United States had remained neutral for several years after the war began, the country was unofficially supporting the British, French, and Russian alliance through trade agreements and financial loans. Sentiment to join the battle began to build after a German submarine sank the *Lusitania*, a British cruise ship with 123 Americans on board, in May 1915. Subsequent threats of more attacks finally led the United States to declare war on Germany on April 6, 1917.

Anti-German sentiment quickly flared in the towns and cities of America. Hamburgers, a reminder of Hamburg, Germany, became Salisbury steak; frankfurters became hot dogs; and sauerkraut became liberty cabbage. More significantly, the acclaimed German-English Academy of Milwaukee became the Milwaukee University School. With the German language widely condemned, German newspapers began to disappear from the newsstands. Fearful of being too closely associated with the enemy, the German Jews of Milwaukee found themselves speaking more English and shifting their sense of patriotism more fully to America. They considered their transition during World War I to be their final step toward assimilation.

By 1917, the Russian Jews no longer resisted aligning with the Allied forces, since the United States' involvement in the war coincided with the overthrow of the czarist regime during the Bolshevik Revolution. Not only were the czars no longer in power, but new leaders in Russia officially outlawed anti-Semitism.

Jews served in large numbers, comprising almost 4 percent of all American forces. More than 225,000 Jewish Americans fought in World War I, including approximately one thousand from Wisconsin. As in any war, the casualties were great. Of the Jewish soldiers that served nationwide, about twelve thousand were wounded, while about 3,500 were killed in action. More than a thousand Jewish American soldiers received awards for meritorious service and bravery, while three received the highest honor awarded to a military soldier—the Congressional Medal of Honor.

As the allegiance to their homeland began to weaken during World War I, Milwaukee's German Jews became more interested in the Zionist movement. Their slowly growing membership in Zionist organizations helped to create a closer bond with their eastern European counterparts. When Hadassah, a women's Zionist organization, was begun in the state by Rachel Jastrow, the sister of the organization's national founder, Henrietta Szold, women of German descent joined with eastern Europeans, strengthening the connection even further.

The dream of a safe Jewish homeland was further encouraged in 1917 when the British signed the Balfour Declaration, asserting Britain's support for a Jewish state in Palestine. If the Allies won the war, Britain avowed that it would be free to carve out a bit of land from the German-allied Ottoman Empire that the United Kingdom would acquire upon victory. However, after Germany signed an armistice agreement on November 11, 1918, thirty more years would pass before a Jewish national homeland was realized, with the establishment of Israel occurring in 1948.

THE CHANGING DEMOGRAPHICS OF SMALL-TOWN WISCONSIN

A community that understands that change is one thing and progress quite another and which is willing to make both happen can succeed and will survive.
—Leonard Zakim, Jewish religious leader

Just as World War I brought about changes in the thinking of Wisconsin's Jews, the postwar period brought about demographic transitions in the Jewish communities of the state's small towns and cities. Many of the German Jewish families living there began to move back to Milwaukee or on to other large cities outside of the state, leaving congregational buildings to be sold to other institutions. While the German Jewish population outside Milwaukee began to shrink, Jews of eastern Europe started to settle in rural areas in greater numbers, joining others of their European origin who had already made the transition. By 1910, the eastern European Jewish population of Milwaukee had grown to twice as large as that of their German forebears. The problems of overcrowding and unemployment only worsened as soldiers returned home. The spread to rural areas was no longer a choice but a vital necessity in the decades after World War I.

The Jewish community of La Crosse was one of the towns that made the demographic transition from German to eastern European during this time. This transition manifested itself physically in the burial grounds. As was the usual case, the early Jewish settlers in small towns made it a priority to buy land for a cemetery, since in the Jewish faith a ritual burial is an important part of paying respect to the deceased. Although the German Jewish settlers of La Crosse first purchased the land, they eventually sold half of it to the eastern European settlers who followed in their path. The tall, opulent tombstones at the German gravesites on one side of the cemetery, compared to the plain, low-lying stone markers of their eastern European coreligionists on the other, reveal a poignant historical contrast between the two groups.

In Green Bay, Jacob Franks and his nephew John Lawe, the earliest Jewish pioneers to arrive in Wisconsin, seemed to have left no trace of their religious heritage by this point. In contrast, by 1884 Aaron Rosenberg, the first Orthodox Jewish man to arrive in the city, had pioneered the way for what was to become a thriving Jewish community.

Other early pioneers of the city, including Azriel Kanter, John Baum, Isaac Cohen, Ben Abrohams, William Sauber, and Sam Abrams, all fled Russia in the 1880s. They became the early pillars in Green Bay's Jewish religious community, which began with services in Aaron Rosenberg's family home to honor the Bar Mitzvah of his son. (See Azriel Kanter's account of leaving Russia in the appendix.) By 1890, 150 Jewish families were working and praying and had become an integral part of the Green Bay culture.

Like most of the Jewish immigrants, the men of Green Bay initially worked as peddlers of fruit, scrap iron, candy, furniture, cattle, and dry goods—enterprises that would eventually morph into businesses that became an important part of the Green Bay economy. However, in the earliest days, the peddlers and their families scrimped and saved their pennies to help pay for an official house of worship. In 1903, when eggs were sixteen cents a dozen and butter was twenty cents a pound, it was a sacrifice to do so. Nevertheless, in that year, the dreams of many became a reality as the cornerstone was laid for the Congregation Cnesses Israel. The first services were held on February 29, 1904. Rebecca Goldman spearheaded the Ladies Aid Society in 1902 to keep the dream alive. Rummage sales, bakery sales, and dues paid by members helped to pay for the needs of the congregation.

Aaron Richman, born in Taverick, Russia, peddled his wares through the streets of New York City when he emigrated in 1881. By

1890, he had made his way to Madison, becoming the first eastern European Jew to venture into the city already occupied by Yankees and German Jewish immigrants. Other eastern European Jews from the same homeland (*landsleit*) followed Richman to the new area. Richman not only led the way to Madison, he also founded the first Orthodox synagogue in the city, Agudas Achim, in 1904. By 1910 more than one hundred Jewish families had joined him.

Many of the Jewish newcomers settled into the Greenbush neighborhood, home to predominantly Italian, Sicilian, Jewish, and African American residents. Bounded by Park Street, Regent Street, and West Washington Avenue, the area dubbed "the Triangle" was home to a cluster of small wood-frame structures and ethnic grocery stores. While walking the streets of the Greenbush neighborhood, one might have savored the aromas of Italian red sauce, baking challah bread, or fried collard greens wafting from adjoining windows. Although the residents may have been some of the poorest in Madison at the time, many of the children who lived there have good memories of growing up in what they fondly refer to as "the Bush."

Madison's Sam Onheiber remembered his childhood at 719 Mound Street with a "soft spot" in his heart. "One of my favorite memories," he recalled, "was that no matter who you were—Jewish, Italian, or Black— you all got along with each other. We never locked our doors and were welcome in one another's homes. . . . If someone had a death in the family but couldn't afford a funeral, all the neighbors would pitch in to pay."

Another longtime resident of the Greenbush neighborhood, Sam Moss, reinforced the nature of the interwoven ethnic groups. Moss, whose parents escaped from Russia in 1905, moved with his family from Milwaukee to Madison's Greenbush neighborhood in 1924 to open a family-run bakery. As he thinks back on his childhood, he affectionately remembers his Italian boyhood friend, Bob Trameri, who was snagged off the street by Mr. Eisenberg, a member of a second Orthodox synagogue, Adas Jeshurun. That day, the congregation needed more men to participate in the Saturday morning minyan. Laughing, Moss recalled that his friend protested, "But I'm a Trameri," questioning the validity of being counted as one of ten required for Hebrew religious prayers since he was Catholic. Mr. Eisenberg retorted, "What's the matter? Are you ashamed of being Jewish?" From then on, his Italian friend began to carry a yarmulke (skullcap worn in a synagogue to show respect to God) in his back pocket for the next time he was needed in an emergency.

One of Madison's most colorful and genial Jewish residents was Solomon Levitan, who was affectionately known by many as "Uncle Sol" for his warm personality. As an immigrant peddler in the early 1880s, Levitan ended up settling in New Glarus. There, he opened a general store, served as justice of the peace, and led religious services at a nearby synagogue in Monroe. When he moved to Madison with his family in 1905, he became involved in the banking business and later became president of the Commercial National Bank. As a good friend and advocate of Governor Bob La Follette, Levitan was known to say more than once, "I sold him a pair of suspenders in the 1880s and have been supporting him ever since." Levitan himself ran for public office and won election to state treasurer for five consecutive two-year terms from 1923 to 1933, and again from 1936 to 1938. In his obituary printed in the *Milwaukee Journal* on February 7, 1940, Levitan was quoted as having said, "Everything I have, I owe to Wisconsin."

As Jewish families sought out life in small-town Wisconsin, the Stevens Point Jewish community grew large enough to establish Temple Beth Israel Congregation. With growing numbers, it became possible to have a kosher cut of meat on the home dinner table, as Alvin Garber, formerly an Arpin resident, became the local *shochet* (someone who supervises the ritual slaughter of an animal). In many small towns, the rabbi might deliver a sermon on Shabbat (the Jewish Sabbath that begins at sundown on Friday and lasts until sundown Saturday) and double as the *shochet* during the week. Both duties are considered very important among Orthodox congregants.

Green Bay's Jewish community also burgeoned, necessitating a larger religious facility. In 1951, a new Congregation Cnesses Israel was erected on Baird Street, this time as a Conservative congregation, modifying the religious rituals of their Orthodox forebears. Its first official religious leader, Rabbi Leonard Goldstein, presided over services as seventy-one Talmud Torah (religious school) students attended classes there.

While Jewish women continued to labor in the home and in the shul (Yiddish word for synagogue), the men often followed their fathers and uncles into the family business. Some, however, took a detour, as was the case with Henry Goldman of Green Bay, who became a pioneer in the motion picture industry after operating a small furniture store on Main

Street. Nathan Abrams was said to have had a hand in getting the Green Bay Packers off the ground in the early 1920s when he temporarily loaned his friend Curly Lambeau three thousand dollars in exchange for the financially struggling franchise. Eventually, Lambeau managed to pay Abrams back by raising money from the general public.

Although not many Jewish men had the time, training, or opportunity to engage in professional sports, the Abrams brothers were among the few exceptions. Nathan Abrams, only five feet four inches in stature, later joined his brother Isadore in playing for the team. He later became president of Green Bay's Community Chest. Another of the few Jewish sports figures of the period emerged from a small town to the north. In the mid-1930s, one of Superior's greatest sports heroes, Morrie "Snooker" Arnovitch, was a major league all-star outfielder who played for the Philadelphia Phillies, the Cincinnati Reds, and the New York Giants. After serving in World War II as an army staff sergeant, he briefly resumed his baseball career before returning to Superior. There, he ran a sporting goods store and became president of the city's Hebrew congregation.

While most Jews strived to maintain a connection to their roots, they simultaneously exerted an effort to become full participants in their new, predominantly Christian communities. Many joined organizations such as the Elks Club, the Chamber of Commerce, the American Legion, and the Jaycees, often assuming leadership roles. Frank's Fruit Store of Green Bay served the townspeople with the sale of Christmas candles; Ben Garber of Stevens Point served as a lay member on the board of St. Michael's Hospital, which was run by Catholic nuns. In fitting with the ecumenical atmosphere that existed, Rabbi Curt Reach of Stevens Point's Beth Israel Congregation would alternate fifteen-minute sermons with other local clergy on radio station WLBL each week.

Most small-town Gentile residents, some of whom had never met a Jewish person before, had a healthy curiosity about their new neighbors. In Stevens Point, a local newspaper, the *Daily Journal*, periodically ran stories about Jewish events, shedding a positive light on the culture and giving details to quench the interest of the townspeople. On November 15, 1904, the *Daily Journal* featured an article about a wedding between two of its Jewish citizens, Louis Zenoff and Lena Fischer. The reporter described the chuppah (canopy under which the bride and groom stand during the ceremony), the seventy-five guests in attendance, and the "bountifully laden supper table." Although the Zenoff family is no longer a presence in Stevens Point, their name remains a familiar one to local residents who enjoy the Zenoff baseball field, named in memory of one of its benefactors.

The peddlers and scrap dealers who had walked the streets of Stevens Point hawking their wares in the early years slowly built up thriving entrepreneurial shops, many of which continued to do business throughout the early 1900s. The Big Shoe, Rudnick's Food Store, Weltman's Grocers, Lipman Furniture, Peacock's Jewelry, and Karp's Bootery were among the 150 small Jewish-owned establishments on the main street and beyond that were frequented by the townspeople.

The *Stevens Point Journal's* obituary of Jewish community leader and business owner A. L. Shafton read, "He was a liberal supporter of all worthy public causes. It is safe to say that Stevens Point has had few, if any, citizens whose private benefactions were as many and varied with such a lack of ostentation as were those of Mr. Shafton. The sadness of the community on the death of Mr. Shafton is deep, genuine, and understandable."

Appleton's Jewish community flourished far beyond its famous names of the 1800s. In 1909, an Orthodox synagogue emerged to accommodate the eastern European Jews who began to move into the city. A small white building with an attached schoolhouse became Moses Montifiore Synagogue, replacing the venue for services that had been held in the home of Sarah and Edward Ressman, early pioneers in the city.

By 1920, 140 members of the Jewish faith made their home in Appleton's welcoming environment, necessitating a larger space. In 1922, the Torah scrolls were ceremoniously carried to a newly constructed brick synagogue with spired roof and stained-glass windows.

Harold Holman, born and raised in Sheboygan, remembers the thriving Jewish community there. His parents were among the nearly one thousand Jewish immigrants who moved there from Lithuania and other eastern European regions now referred to as Belarus. Word traveled from the earliest settlers that Sheboygan was a place to find jobs and a secure life for their children. Like so many others, Holman's father peddled scrap metal and later fruit through the streets of the city, while his mother prepared food for events held within the Jewish community. Holman fondly remembers his mother's tzimmes (sweet fruit and potato stew), *p'tcha* (gelatin made from calves feet), and blintzes (thin rolled pancakes often filled with cheese), all dishes familiar to those who had lived in her region of the Old Country. Even though his parents and most of the older Jewish generation spoke Yiddish and prepared foods from their shtetl past, Holman felt very much a part of the Sheboygan landscape. In grade school he made good friends with Jews and non-Jews alike. After serving in the army, he and his wife, who hailed from Brooklyn, New York, returned to Sheboygan. As an active member of both his synagogue and the city, Holman enjoyed several leadership roles in Sheboygan. He became an enthusiastic member of the Optimist Club, served on the fund-raising board for a local nursing home, and was active in the Veterans Association for fifty years as of 2015.

While most Jews in small Wisconsin cities survived and even thrived in the first half of the 1900s, many felt an internal conflict between assimilating to the world around them and clinging to their Jewish heritage. Some felt it wasn't possible to do both and ended up joining Christian churches. Others felt that it was up to them to represent Judaism in the best light possible and made strong commitments to maintain their religious practices. At times, such commitment entailed traveling long distances for their children's religious education, attending religious services at out-of-town synagogues, and having kosher meat shipped in from larger Jewish hubs.

Recognizing the yearnings to have young teens maintain their Jewish identity, B'nai B'rith offered youth organizations, such as Aleph Zadik Aleph (AZA) for boys and B'nai B'rith Girls (BBG) for girls, in almost every city where a Jewish population existed. Under the umbrella B'nai B'rith Youth Organization (BBYO), these groups brought young people of both genders together at regional conferences to engage in youth leadership programs and gain a greater understanding of their Jewish roots. Summer camps, such as Camp Ramah in Conover, Wisconsin; Olin Sang Ruby in Oconomowoc; and Camp Interlaken in Eagle River began to crop up, each representing either an Orthodox, Conservative, or Reform orientation. All these programs encouraged a connection to Judaism through sports, arts, and long-lasting friendships.

Despite some difficulties involved in living a Jewish life in small towns, the more plentiful successes and pleasant experiences kept Jewish families there throughout the early to mid-1900s. By 1920, a thriving

Jewish presence could be found in 241 Wisconsin communities. Changes that would take place in the second half of the century would create demographic shifts that no one could have imagined as they were establishing roots in their small towns throughout the state.

THE ROARING TWENTIES

*How does one understand—not even forgive, simply understand—
the virulent anti-Semitic statements of intellectuals throughout history?*
—Professor Alan Dershowitz

The post–World War I era brought the German and eastern European Jews closer together in spirit than any other time since their arrival in the United States. The eastern Europeans had become more assimilated to the American way of life, and the Germans felt free to become more overtly Jewish. Both groups were enjoying a sense of stability, success, and national pride, which reflected the country's attitude as a whole.

However, throughout the 1920s, great swings of fortune and misfortune affected American society, which had a total population of 106 million as the decade began. Of those, approximately 30,000 Jews were living in Wisconsin, out of 3.5 million of the Jewish faith who resided in the country at large. Although relative prosperity ushered in the 1920s, it was not to last. As new immigrants from all parts of the world rushed to America's doors, crime and poverty rapidly increased, in many cases involving newcomers who struggled to survive by engaging in illegal activities. Irish, Italian, and Jewish Mafias arose in the overcrowded tenements of New York.

The time was ripe for the Ku Klux Klan to reemerge, spreading their anti-"other" gospel—this time directed as much toward Jews, Irish, and Catholics as toward African Americans during the Civil War period. The Klan was not alone in spewing hateful rhetoric. Henry Ford, one of the most influential industrialists of the time, was also one of the most dominant anti-Semitic voices. Through a newspaper, the *Dearborn Independent*, and pamphlets distributed to buyers of the popular Model T cars, Ford attempted to spread his belief that Jews were about to take over the economic and political world through secret societies. He also claimed that Jews were conspiring to control the world's banking and media, in spite of the fact that Jews represented a very small minority in both professions.

The influence of Ford and other prominent anti-Semites ignited pockets of prejudice against Jews in areas around the country, including in Milwaukee and other Wisconsin cities. Often Jewish vacationers were met with the word "restricted" at Wisconsin hotels, motels, and resorts. The brochure for the Wildwood Resort in Lac du Flambeau extolled the fact that it was "a wholesome well-ordered resort where comfort, pleasant companionship and good service are the outstanding features. . . . Our policy does not permit any except Gentiles, no undesirables ever are entertained."

In a September 1993 issue of *Milwaukee Magazine*, Marty Stein, one of that city's most generous philanthropists, recalled that when his parents looked for a place to rent in the 1920s, they encountered blunt messages that read, "No dogs and no Jews." Stein also remembered being "beaten up on my way home from Hebrew school."

Although many social organizations in Milwaukee were closed to Jews, Jewish leaders began to organize their own gathering places. Brynwood Country Club, which opened in 1929, was one example. Although its membership was open to Jews and non-Jews, the majority of the two hundred families that joined were of German Jewish descent. Before long, more than one hundred different Jewish social, educational, and charitable organizations existed in the city that at the time housed twenty-two thousand Jewish residents—4 percent of the total population.

In addition to blaming Jews and other immigrants for the wrongs of society, many people in the country blamed the rampant crime on the consumption of alcohol. Under pressure from the Anti-Salon League and some Protestant groups called the "drys," President Woodrow Wilson signed the Prohibition Act into law in 1920. The law made it illegal to buy, sell, or consume liquor in any public place. Rather than lessening crime, however, Prohibition inspired new lucrative criminal pursuits in venues called "speakeasies," where liquor was sold illegally.

Wisconsin was hit particularly hard by Prohibition. By then Milwaukee had established itself as the beer capital of the country. The breweries that were started by early Gentile German immigrants, such as Pabst, Schlitz, and Blatz, contributed to making the manufacture of beer the fifth-largest industry in the state. In domino fashion, the industry's total collapse also severely affected the half of the state's population who made their living through farming, since barley used in beer had become an important cash crop. Milwaukee continued to represent one-third of the state's industrial output, with auto parts production, meat-packing, and leather foundry products leading the way. But many Jews and other immigrants who owned small liquor stores, as well as farmers who tilled the land, suffered greatly from Prohibition's effects.

Despite the influences of Prohibition and the rising anti-Semitism in much of the country, the early 1920s were transformative for the Jews of Wisconsin. The Jewish immigrants of eastern Europe felt a sense of physical safety and freedom in America that they had never known in the past.

Hilda and Sam Gross, who fled Russia in 1908 to escape the brutality of the pogroms and conscription into the army, settled in Viroqua. Years later, Hilda wrote this in a letter, extolling her feelings about being an American: "To stand where you can stand in the middle of the street and look up to the bright sky and really feel that you belong here . . . I thank God every day for that. Yes, I am free, as free as can be."

As eastern European Jews began to earn a living and develop a sense of confidence that they belonged in the United States, they gradually abandoned the crowded quarters of Milwaukee's Haymarket district and headed northwest to a more suburban setting. Duplexes and bungalows that lined the streets of a four-square-mile community called Sherman Park replaced the ramshackle buildings they left behind. A lucky few even had a garage in case they could one day afford an automobile. As was often the case, the eastern Europeans' move toward a better life seemed to follow the upward mobility of their German predecessors, who had headed further east toward Milwaukee's lakeshore.

For the most part, German and Russian Jews alike decided to focus on education as a way to alleviate poverty and to counter accusations bred by anti-Semitism. For eastern European Jews, the schools of Sherman Park offered their children a better education than they would have gotten in Haymarket. In addition to providing instruction, Sherman Elementary and Washington High School escalated assimilation for their offspring. A boy with a name such as Fival became Frank to his classmates. Shima became Susan. Before long, the English language replaced any remnants of Yiddish that had lingered on the tongues of the second generation.

By the early 1920s, the educated children of the first-generation ped-dlers were well prepared to enter colleges, universities, and professional schools, making it possible to fulfill the immigrant generation's ever-pre-sent dream of higher education. Although Jews represented 3 percent of the country's population, the numbers of Jewish students in medical and law schools far exceeded that proportion. As the decade began, many possessed an optimism that the new economic prosperity and educa-tional opportunities would last.

THE DOOR SHUTS TIGHTLY

A vision is inspired by your belief about human possibility, while being influenced by your experience of human fallibility.
—Seymour Fox, Jewish educator

Despite the movement of many immigrants out of large cities, lessening the overcrowded conditions, many Americans wanted to limit the number of refugees entering the country, particularly eastern Europeans. By 1920, 3.2 million Jews were living in the United States. Most were of Russian descent and resided in the most populated Eastern and Mid-western cities. By then, Milwaukee was home to the ninth-largest Jewish population in the country.

Bowing to the will of many citizens, the US Congress passed the Immigration Act of 1921. Signed by President Warren Harding, the law severely limited the number of eastern European refugees entering the country. As stringent as those restrictions seemed, pressure continued to mount for legislators to close the door even more tightly. The Johnson Reed Immigration Act of 1924 accomplished that goal by limiting the entry of immigrants from a particular country to just 2 percent of that country's existing US population, as of the 1890 census. In effect, it greatly limited the entry of Jews, since a comparatively small Jewish pop-ulation had settled in the United States by the 1890 date.

Wisconsin activists such as Polish cleric Father Waclaw Kruszka and Joseph Padway, a Jewish attorney in Milwaukee, led a band of protest-ers, proclaiming, "God's country belongs to all." Their voices were drowned out as the quota system continued, with a 20 percent decrease in immigration in 1924 as compared to the pre–World War I average.

Eventually such quotas spread to college campuses and professional schools throughout the United States, limiting the number of Jewish students who could be accepted for admittance at one time. The enrollment of Jewish students, particularly at Ivy League schools, quickly shrank. The number of Jewish college professors fell from 8 percent in 1917 to less than 2 percent in 1929 as faculty appointments for Jews became rarer. Columbia's College of Physicians and Surgeons' Jewish enrollment dipped from 50 percent in 1923 to 6 percent in 1939. Those who were lucky enough to graduate from professional schools were often stopped in their tracks when they were not admitted to hospital residency programs or were unable to find jobs in their field.

The University of Wisconsin (UW) did not impose the same quotas that were set by many East Coast and Midwestern institutions, which had sharply limited the number of Jewish students. Wisconsin governor Robert M. La Follette had envisioned and proposed legislation to make the university campus more diverse and open to students from beyond Wisconsin's borders. In the late 1920s, the UW campus became a haven for second- and third-generation Jewish offspring from inside and outside the state. To accommodate their needs, the Hillel Foundation (Jewish student organization) opened its second chapter at the university in 1924, one year after it was first established at the University of Illinois.

La Crosse County Historical Society

La Crosse Public Library Archives Department
and La Crosse County Historical Society

Born in Wurtemberg, Germany, in 1840, Albert Hirshheimer resided in La Crosse from 1856 to his death in 1924. In 1865 he bought a small plow shop and built it into a successful agricultural manufacturer.

John Levy, the first Jewish resident of La Crosse, arrived in 1845 and became mayor of the city in 1850. In addition to being a civic leader, Levy was a fur trader, merchant, real estate developer, and financier.

Slinger Community Library

In 1851, Baruch Schleisinger Weil founded the town of Schleisingerville, later renamed Slinger. He was elected as a state senator in 1852 and was appointed brigadier general of the state militia in 1856.

WHi Image ID 5103

Samuel Klauber, one of the first Jewish residents of Madison, arrived in 1851 and soon became a religious and civic leader in the city.

WHi Image ID 52779

The adult children of Samuel Klauber are pictured in 1910. Moses Klauber took over the family business in Madison while his sisters Lena (left) and Sophia (right) relocated to Buffalo, New York.

Lizzie Black Kander founded the Settlement in Milwaukee to aid eastern European immigrants and later wrote *The Settlement Cookbook* as a fundraiser. Reprints of her cookbook can still be found in kitchens across the country.

WHi Image ID 38113

Marc Cohen

Harry Houdini's father, Rabbi Mayer Samuel Weiss, presided over the former Temple Zion in Appleton beginning in 1883.

Mark Seiler/Portage County Historical Society

Alvin Garber emigrated from Russia in 1913. He served the important roles of both rabbi and *shochet* (one who supervises the kosher ritual slaughter of animals) in Stevens Point.

Israel and Dora Shafton, pictured with sons A. B. and S. Mendel circa 1899. Israel Shafton immigrated to Milwaukee in 1891 and then settled in Stevens Point, where his family joined him in 1899. He was one of the founders and the first president of the Beth Israel congregation there.

Mark Seiler/Portage County Historical Society

Isaac Bunin, brother-in-law to Israel Shafton, is pictured with his wife, Chaye, and their four children, Sonia, Pearl, Samuel, and Rose, circa 1900. Bunin helped found the Beth Israel congregation and operated Bunin & Sons Dry Goods in Stevens Point until 1941.

Mark Seiler/Portage County Historical Society

Jewish Museum Milwaukee

Abraham Forman, at his Bar Mitzvah in 1917 wears *tefillin*, an armband containing verses from the Torah used by Orthodox Jews during prayer. After graduating from the University of Wisconsin and Marquette Medical School, Forman practiced medicine in Milwaukee until his death at age forty.

WHi Image ID 5348

A performance of Poale Zion Chasidim, an Americanization pageant that was performed at the Milwaukee Auditorium to welcome new citizens to Milwaukee in 1919. The woman wearing the white blouse is believed to be Golda Meir, future prime minister of Israel.

WHi Image ID 37073

A group gathered for a Zionist event in Milwaukee in 1925. Milwaukee became a Zionist hub in the early 1900s.

Jewish Museum Milwaukee

The wedding party of Harry Sokol and Bess Klieger in Milwaukee in the mid-1920s.

Sylvia Grunes

Young members of the Workman's Circle (Arbeiter Ring) gave many plays that espoused their philosophy. Madison resident Sylvia Grunes is in the top row, fifth from the left, in this play performed circa 1945.

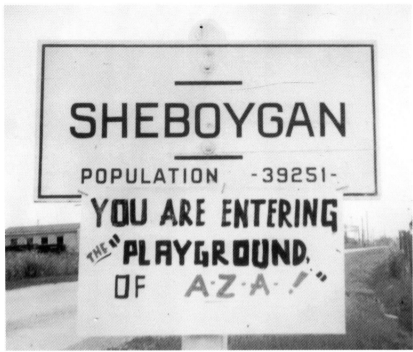

Joel Alpert

Sheboygan played host to one of the many Wisconsin AZA conferences. This sign attached to the city's marker in 1937 welcomed young men from around the state to the conference.

TROUBLE BREWING

Fear is the main source of superstition, and one of the main
sources of cruelty. To conquer fear is the beginning of wisdom.
—Bertrand Russell

As the 1920s drew to a close, prosperous economic times were beginning to change in Wisconsin. The earliest troubles began in the rural areas of the state, where 50 percent of the population resided. World War I had been a boon for farmers who had supplied food during the war effort. But after the war, the demand for surplus food that had been produced dropped with a thud, as did the income of many farmers. In 1920, a cow sold for thirty-eight dollars. By 1929, the same cow would bring in only three dollars at market.

As agricultural prosperity faded in the nation, so too did the purchasing power of half the state's population, while postwar inflation continued. Farmers began to leave their land but were often unable to find work in urban areas. By the end of the 1920s, people had less disposable income and therefore less ability to buy goods, greatly impacting industry. Such conditions were factors leading up to the Great Depression.

President Herbert Hoover, elected in 1928, recognized the rising economic problems but advocated a hands-off approach, believing that the recession would right itself. On October 29, 1929, he was proven terribly wrong when the stock market crashed. Many Americans lost their entire savings, kept in banks that had invested their money in the market. People panicked, withdrawing whatever money they could. By 1933, seven thousand banks throughout the country had failed as a result.

From 1930 to 1931, wages declined by 40 percent in the United States. Unemployment rose from 4 to 18 percent. By 1932, many family farms and homes were in foreclosure. And in 1933, 34 percent of the workforce was unemployed. Wisconsin reflected the economic woes of the nation, with a 60 percent decline in wages from 1929 to 1930. By 1934, 50 percent of Wisconsin's population was receiving government assistance. Those who didn't have enough money to buy food buried their pride and stood in long soup lines to receive free rations.

Often when the economy was in trouble, Jews were blamed, and the 1930s proved no exception. No longer did a so-called enlightened society

claim that Jews used the blood of Gentile children in their religious rituals, but many were easily convinced that Jews were responsible for bringing the economy to its knees. Father Charles Coughlin, a Catholic priest
from Canada with a pulpit in Royal Oak, Michigan, used his weekly
radio ministry to spread his anti-Semitic views that were closely tied to
the birth of modern anti-Semitism in Germany. Father Coughlin hit the
airwaves in 1926, attracting a small group of listeners as he spoke to the
hopes and fears of people who were struggling to make a living. By the
1930s, his ministry was broadcast to a vast audience, including listeners
of radio station WIBA in Wisconsin. They heard him warn of the need
to be suspicious of Jews. In 1936 he followed up his radio accusations by
distributing a paper called "Social Justice," which declared that Jews
were in control of the country's financial institutions. But not everyone
accepted Father Coughlin's words as the truth. The *Wisconsin State Journal* reported on December 15, 1938, that the members of the Madison
Council for Liberal Action voted to ask WIBA to keep Coughlin's broad-
casts off the air, calling them "a menace to democratic institutions."

ON ANOTHER FRONT:
THE MAKING OF WORLD WAR II

Even the most peaceful of men can feel exultation
on the threshold of a just war.
—US Senator Jacob R. Javitz

Simultaneous to a growing distrust of American Jews, Adolf Hitler came
to power as the head of the Nazi party in Germany—a country that was
also undergoing an economic depression in 1933. Gradually the Nazis
stripped Germany's 523,000 Jews, 1 percent of its total population, of
their rights, their homes, and their livelihoods. As the Nazis focused on
eradicating anyone who did not possess pure Aryan blood, Jews were
forced to distinguish themselves by wearing a yellow Star of David armband. On November 9–10, 1938, German troopers attacked Jews in their
homes and businesses, crashing through glass windows and arresting
every Jew they could find.

Kristallnacht (Crystal Night), named for the large amount of shattered glass, was a tremendously loud wakeup call for those Jews who still believed that their freedoms would eventually be restored when the Nazis were out of power. Those who saw the future more clearly made arrangements to leave with the help of friends and relatives in other countries. By 1939, when it was still possible to leave Germany and Austria, approximately three hundred thousand Jews left for places such as Palestine, Argentina, and the United States. More than four hundred Jewish refugees from Germany made their way to Milwaukee and other Wisconsin cities that year.

Although President Franklin D. Roosevelt was sympathetic to the Jewish plight, the US government did little to help the Jews seek refuge in the United States during the war due to stringent immigration quotas that were still in effect. On May 13, 1939, 930 Jewish refugees boarded the ocean liner SS *St. Louis* in Hamburg, Germany, bound for Havana, Cuba. Upon arrival, they thought they would seek visas to the United States. But when the ocean liner arrived in Havana two weeks later, the Jewish refugees were denied entrance. With their hopes dashed, the passengers clung to the possibility of sailing the short distance to Florida's shore, where they might be allowed entry into the United States. However, upon their arrival there, the US Coast Guard refused to let the ship stay. The group was forced to sail back to Europe, where countries other than Germany allowed them to enter.

By 1941 it was no longer possible for Jews to leave Germany, as the Nazi leaders had come up with another plan to rid their country of its Jewish population. Their next strategy was known as the "Final Solution." From that point on, Jewish men, women, and children were loaded onto trains and taken to concentration camps with their specially designed gas chambers and incinerators where millions perished. More than 617 of the once hopeful passengers of the SS *St. Louis* eventually died as one by one, the places in which they had sought refuge came under Nazi occupation. In spite of the strict US immigration quotas at the time, a bill was brought before Congress to admit twenty thousand Jewish children into the country, above the prescribed limit. But both houses of Congress allowed the proposed legislation to die.

Fortunately, Nicholas Winton, a Christian businessman from Britain, recognized the grave need to help Jewish children of the Czecho-Slovak Republic leave for safety as German troops were advancing to occupy their country. Through meticulous research and energetic fund-raising,

Winton and many other volunteers listed hundreds of Jewish children who would need to leave their homes for London, provided they could find a family who was willing to take them in. The British government quickly approved of the *Kindertransport* plan. Renata Laxova (nee Polgar), a Madison resident and emeritus professor of pediatric genetics at the University of Wisconsin Medical School, was one of those children. By the spring of 1939, the Nazis had made their way to the city of Brno, in the Czech portion of the republics, where Renata had lived a "secure and peaceful" life with her parents. Realizing the danger to her only child, Renata's mother scrambled to secure passage on the *Kindertransport* train to England and find a family that was willing to offer her daughter a place in their home. On July 31, eight-year-old Renata left her parents and everything that was familiar to her as she climbed aboard the last of eight trains that transported a total of 669 children out of their homeland to safety. "I always knew my parents weren't coming with me," she recalls, "but in the car, on the way to the train station, it really hit me. I began to cry and beg my parents not to send me, bargaining that, from then on, I would eat my spinach." With tears in their eyes, her parents told her, "It's because we love you that we're sending you away."

For years, Renata's only communication with her parents was through letters, which she has saved in cardboard boxes through the years. Other treasured letters came from caring friends of the family who wrote to ease the little girl's homesickness. One such message came from Renata's favorite dog, Burry, written by his owner, Ms. Blum, who had tutored Renata in English before she left for England. The letter read in part, "I am always looking for your door, hoping that Renata will come out and call me." Shortly after the letter arrived, the Germans decreed that Jews were not allowed to own domestic pets or farm animals. Renata later learned that both Burry and his owner had perished during the Holocaust.

By 1941, such forms of communication were forbidden. Throughout the remainder of the war, only brief twenty-five-word lettergrams were sent back and forth through underground organizations in Europe or the Red Cross in the United States.

Following seven years in the country home of a caring Quaker family by the name of Daniels, Renata reunited with both of her parents when the war ended. To her knowledge, only five of the 669 children who had been sent to England through the *Kindertransport* program were able to rejoin both their parents. Those who were reunited with at least one parent were considered lucky, since so many people who were forbidden to leave perished in concentration camps. In later life, Renata traveled to Wisconsin to accept a position at the University of Wisconsin's medical school. When she married and had her first child, she named her Daniela, in honor of the family that had saved her life.

Albert Beder of Milwaukee was not as lucky. Born in Kaumus, Lithuania, he attended a youth camp in Palanga for both Jewish and Lithuanian children in the summer of 1941 at age thirteen. It was near the German border. He arrived at the camp on June 15 and vividly recalls what happened just a few days later:

> On June 22, at four in the morning we heard shots being fired less than a mile away. Someone came in to where the children were sleeping and shouted, "Get dressed." The German soldiers had neared the campsite. All the children tried to run but we were caught and brought back to the camp. The next day the 100 Jewish children were separated from the others and led to a marketplace guarded by both German and Lithuanian soldiers with rifles. We joined about 150 adult Jews who had been rounded up from the city. This act was referred to as an *aktion* [German word for action taken]. There was chaos. A leader of the German troops called out, "All men from seventeen to fifty-five step forward." That group was loaded onto two large trucks that drove away. No one knew where they were headed. About one-half hour later a Lithuanian woman shouted from across the street, "They shot the men!" The soldiers then jammed children and adults into a small space in the synagogue. The stench of all those frightened people huddled together was terrible. Then there was an order that all Jews had to be transferred to a ghetto by August 15. Over 300 people were forced into a schoolhouse with ten families living in one class. There was no running water, no sanitation, and no place to cook or bathe. The Germans quickly moved among the people there, demanding anything valuable that a person may have. Anyone who refused to give away a special possession would be shot. Next, everyone was taken to a field that was called "Democrato." There we were sorted into two different groups. In a split second, one

officer decided the fate of hundreds of people. If he pointed to the right, you were a goner. To the left, you were sent to work for the Nazi war effort. I was sent to work building heavy concrete walls for an underground airfield. I got two loaves of bread for the work to help support my family. During that time, all the Jews in another small ghetto town of Vilne were killed. Other Jews tried to run and get to Russia. My little sister Riva, six years old, tried to run and got lost. In the town of Slabotke, the Lithuanians killed 860 Jews before the Germans had arrived.

By 1942, things seemed to be calming down. Jews were allowed to grow vegetables and the killing had subsided. But one day in October, we were ordered to report to the gate of the ghetto with only the clothes on our backs. They took us to Riga, a labor camp run by Lutov, the German air force, where I worked until 1943. That year my father was taken away and died. I was then taken to Schtreoff. At that point I had to say good-bye to my mother and sisters and leave all clothes and possessions behind. I was given a striped shirt and pants in Barrack 17 where we were pushed in like chickens. By the time I was sixteen years old, I was transferred to one of the Dachau camps, number ten. A total of 550 people slept there in bunkers three feet underground with a roof on top. I was assigned to a concrete factory. At first we were given one loaf of bread for ten people and watery soup twice a day. By December, we only got soup at night and a loaf of bread for fourteen people. The greatest suffering came in January, February, and March of 1945. Many people starved to death. Some officers would say to those who were living, "We will kill you before this is over."

On April 20 of that year, we were given orders to go to the main camp of Dachau. As we were marched from one place to another, we passed hundreds of dead bodies lying on the ground. When we reported to the gate we were given a piece of bread and one issue of canned meat. From there, we were marched for 10 days to Innsbruck. People were so starved that some stopped to eat a dead horse lying on the side of the road. I thought that this would be the end for me as I blanked out from hunger and exhaustion. And it would have been if not for one officer's German shepherd dog who began nipping at my leg. Its bites woke me up. Otherwise I would have been shot for not being able to carry on. Then on May 1 we were marched into an open field covered with snow. We found out that the Americans had landed. We were laughing and crying at the same time. You can't imagine what it's like to be taken from the lion's mouth. My sisters were at another camp and liberated by the Russians.

Although most citizens in countries of Nazi occupation chose silence and inaction for their own protection, others performed great acts of bravery and courage to try to save their Jewish neighbors. At their own peril those known as the "righteous" concealed families in their homes, smuggled food and necessities to those in hiding, or joined underground groups that did what they could to stave off the brutal murders of their countrymen. Waclaw Szybalski was one such person. Szybalski, an emeritus professor of oncology, was lured to Wisconsin after the war to accept a position at the University of Wisconsin's McArdle Laboratory for Cancer Research. Although he became known for his groundbreaking discoveries that include the first creation of functional DNA in a petri dish, Szybalski's scientific accomplishments are matched by his humanitarian deeds during the war.

Born in 1921 in Lwow, Poland, to a Catholic family, Szybalski spoke of his strong ties to both Jews and non-Jews throughout his school years and beyond. Before the war, Lwow, historically a city of one-quarter million, was approximately 25 percent Jewish and 60 percent Catholic. "Classmates of the two faiths easily mingled," Szybalski recalled. But he remembers how "things changed completely" in September 1939, when the Soviet Russians overran the city, progressively arresting selected classes of the population and eventually killing large numbers of political prisoners.

When the Germans invaded less than three years later, in July 1941, they quickly "rounded up Jews house by house and transferred them to crowded ghettos of the city." Although the ghettos remained open at first, "Suddenly one night in 1941, all of them were closed by order of the Gestapo." Gradually Jews were transported to Belzec and Janowska concentration camps outside of town. Like his father, a young Szybalski joined the Polish underground. Given his youth and keen intelligence, he was delegated to penetrate Belzec to find out what was happening there. In the summer of 1943, he and another underground member, Hanka

Wroblewska, took off on their bikes, rode sixty miles, and hiked through forests. They eventually hid for four days in a local school, where they were helped by a member of Zegota (a special branch of the Polish underground army devoted to helping Jews). From their hiding spot, they were able to get a full view of the camp's grounds. "We saw trains arriving and people being chased down from the train," Szybalski recalls. "We saw hundreds, maybe thousands, of bodies being burned and could smell the unforgettable, repulsive odor of burning flesh that permeated the air. . . . We realized what was taking place." The two young men set to work making intricate drawings of the camp and train tracks. When they returned with their maps, others in the underground planned to blow up the tracks with TNT to forestall the transport of Jews and other victims of the Nazis. Jan Karski, an officer of the Polish underground, brought the plans to Winston Churchill and then to President Roosevelt in the United States. Both leaders decided against the strategy, feeling that their main mission was to "win the war and deal with the Holocaust later."

As the war continued, Szybalski trained as a chemist. His new skills enabled him to work in the lab of the renowned scientist Rudolph Weigl, who discovered the first effective typhus vaccine in the 1920s. Because typhus was a virulent disease carried by lice, the Nazis ordered the lab to make great amounts of the vaccine for their troops, who lived in close quarters and often didn't have time to bathe. Unknown to the German officials, underground workers in the lab made sure that the soldiers received a diluted strain of the vaccine, while they managed to smuggle the full strain into the concentration camps where typhus was prevalent. "We would pack the ampules and carry them by train," Szybalski remembers. "If I had been discovered, I would have been shot right on the spot. During the entire war, I felt like a rabbit during hunting season." In German-occupied Poland, anyone helping Jews faced the death penalty.

Despite the brave work of Waclaw Szybalski and others who risked their lives to help the 3.5 million Jews who had lived in Poland before the war, over 3 million perished by its end.

Others throughout war-torn Europe opened their homes to hide, and thus save, people such as Jewish refugee Martin Deutschkron. After surviving Kristallnacht, German work camps, and two years of fearful hiding, Deutschkron eventually came to live in Madison, Wisconsin, under the

sponsorship of residents Herman and Fannie Mack, leaders in the Jewish community. Once in the United States, Deutschkron and his wife,
Eva, established themselves in Madison. Martin became a successful
tailor who owned a shop at 427 State Street. In 1977 he was asked to
speak publicly about his experiences during the war (see appendix).

In sharp contrast to the so-called righteous individuals of Europe
and generous sponsors of refugees in the United States, some groups in
big cities organized and aligned themselves with Hitler's ideology. The
German-American Bund, which was first called "Friends of New Germany," began in New York in 1933 and spread to Wisconsin in 1934,
attracting approximately five hundred members soon after. Dressed in
uniforms that resembled those of Nazi troopers, the members held ral-
lies, demonstrations, and parades at which they echoed Hitler's white
Aryan supremacy ideology. As in Germany, the youth were considered
very important in furthering the white-Aryan cause. With that in mind,
the German-American Bund of Wisconsin opened Camp Hindenburg
in May 1940. On the peaceful banks of the Milwaukee River in the little
town of Grafton, young children were taught to march in lockstep and
salute the Führer while decked out in drab brown shirts and highly pol-
ished boots. In an effort to distance itself from the German-American
Bund, the Federation of German American Societies banned Bund
members from their organization. They distinguished themselves further
by leasing land from Camp Hindenburg and establishing Camp Carl
Schurz, a place that represented the philosophical opposite of its Bund
predecessor. German parents who did not support the Bund cause were
assured that "no flag but the stars and stripes" would fly there and that
their children would not be taught pro-Nazi dogma.

Despite the attempts of the Federation of German-American Societies
to weaken the Bund, the split over support for Hitler among Milwaukee residents of German descent bubbled over long before the United States officially entered the war. Riots broke out on the streets of the city during two
separate Bund demonstrations, provoking a strong response. On May 27,
1939, five thousand Wisconsinites—Jews and Gentiles alike—gathered for
an anti-Hitler rally at the Milwaukee Auditorium.

When Hitler's goals of German supremacy led to the invasion and
occupation of Austria, Czechoslovakia, and Poland, the United States'
involvement in World War II was becoming inevitable. However, President Roosevelt's 1940 campaign slogans for reelection to a third term

echoed the isolationist mood of the country. It was not unusual for crowds to greet him at his campaign stops hoisting signs that read, "Keep us out of War." Such a request was not to be realized. Two days after Germany's ally, Japan, attacked the US naval base Pearl Harbor on December 7, 1941, the United States became a full participant in the battle which was to become one of the most destructive events in human history.

Out of the sixteen million Americans who served in the armed forces in World War II, 550,000 were Jewish, many of them volunteering for duty. One of the most highly recognized soldiers from Wisconsin was Leonard Bessman of Milwaukee, who fought in some of the harshest battles in the North African Theater. On April 7, 1943, Bessman, a lieutenant in the counterintelligence corps, was leading the way for an army unit that was advancing toward enemy territory in Tunisia. He soon found himself cut off from the others as a German armed tank appeared before him. Thinking of his fellow soldiers who were trailing behind, he held the enemy driver under cover with his machine gun, shouting, "Come on out and I won't shoot," as he sent warning to his commander not to advance any farther. Putting himself in the line of enemy fire, Bessman was shot and taken prisoner.

After Bessman's capture by the Germans, he was placed in a POW camp in Chieti, Italy, where he remained for two months until he and two other captives maneuvered a daring escape. After traveling by night and hiding by day, they made their way to the Italian village of Pescara, still fearing that their recapture might be inevitable since the Germans then occupied Italy. To their good fortune, a kind Italian farmer offered to hide the men in a small shack behind his house until it was safer for them to leave.

After nearly six months of being hidden by a series of Italian families, Bessman and the two others decided that they could risk returning to the Allied line with the aid of an organization formed by US and British intelligence to help escapees. Once back with Allied forces, the soldiers were able to divulge important information regarding German whereabouts that they had learned from their time within enemy-occupied territory. Although no longer in Italy, none of the men would ever forget the courageous Italian families who took great risks to save the soldiers' lives.

Following a debriefing about his experiences at the US Pentagon,

Bessman returned to the European Theater to help liberate those held at the Buchenwald concentration camp in Germany. Before the war's end, he was promoted to the rank of lieutenant colonel, personally receiving the Distinguished Service Cross from five-star general Omar Bradley for his bravery. He was also decorated with the Silver Star and the Purple Heart with clusters. Known throughout the army ranks for his heroism, Bessman was later recognized in General Bradley's memoirs. Ernie Pyle, the famed war correspondent, also singled him out in his book *This Is Your War*. He wrote of Bessman: "Of all the soldiers I have ever known, he is the most sensitive to the little beauties of war and the big tragedies of life . . . his bravery was a byword among us."

On May 8, 1945, the war ended in Europe with Hitler's defeat. On September 2 of the same year, Japan surrendered. By the war's end, twenty-six thousand Jewish men and women who fought in the US military were cited for valor and merit. Eleven thousand had been killed. Those who returned were haunted by the tragic end that befell their European counterparts. During the Holocaust, 70 percent of Europe's Jewish population—six million Jews, including an estimated one million children—had been slaughtered, been suffocated in gas chambers, or wasted away in Nazi concentration camps. Some of the survivors ended up finding their way to Wisconsin.

BACK HOME

For the dead and the living, we must bear witness.
—Eli Weisel, author and Holocaust survivor

The victory in World War II instilled a new sense of pride in the American psyche. The Great Depression ended, and the United States, less than two hundred years old, had assumed the status of the world's superpower in what was commonly referred to as the country's golden age. The postwar era was an optimistic period for Jews and non-Jews alike. Life had settled down into a certain domestic routine, greatly valued after the chaos of family separations during wartime. With only 1.8 percent unemployment throughout the country in 1946, the promise of a peaceful and prosperous future lay ahead.

For the Jewish population in the United States, the situation seemed particularly hopeful. In addition to a sense of economic prosperity, Jews experienced a new sense of comfort as overt anti-Semitism began to decline. When photos of emaciated death camp survivors and heaps of gassed bodies reached the US media, the nation as a whole became more supportive of the Jewish plight.

Unfortunately, small pockets of overt discrimination remained. One example could be seen in a leaflet of the Dell View Hotel in the Wisconsin Dells, distributed to the Wisconsin Bar Association before it held its 1946 conference there. It warned, "Clientele is restricted," code for not allowing African Americans or Jews to enter.

Far more upsetting, many Jews living in the United States had their greatest fears confirmed when they learned that members of their families had been killed in the Holocaust. Those who had surviving relatives feverishly tried to help them secure safety. Although many of the people liberated from slave labor and death camps were repatriated to their home countries, many did not want to live among their tormentors. Instead, most Jewish survivors of the Holocaust went to temporary camps and became known as DPs (displaced persons) needing to find a new place to call home. Despite the British Balfour Declaration of 1917, which promised a Jewish homeland in Palestine, Britain did a complete turnaround during World War II. In 1939, the British government issued a document known as the White Paper, designed to appease its Arab war allies by barring all Jewish DPs from entering Palestinian territory that had come under British control after World War I.

In the United States, several DP bills were proposed, repealed, and revised. Alexander Wiley, the US Senator representing Wisconsin, proposed a bill stipulating a December 1945 cutoff date for entering the country. Such a time limitation would have excluded all those who, in 1946, had to flee Communist and anti-Semitic terror in Poland, which persisted after the war ended. The Honorable Judge Charles Aarons of the Second Judicial Circuit Court of Milwaukee wrote a letter urging Senator Wiley, Senator Joseph McCarthy, and other legislators to change the date to April 21, 1947:

July 28, 1948
Senator Alexander Wiley
Senate Office Building
Washington, D.C.

Dear Senator:

I have written you in the past about the so-called DP Bills. The Act which was passed—known as the "Wiley Act"—is seriously deficient for reasons that have been probably brought to your attention.

I wish particularly to call your attention to the so-called "cutoff" date, which is December 27, 1945 and which in the Act as passed excludes all those who fled from Communist and Anti-Semitic terror in Poland in 1946. I strongly urge that the "cutoff" date be changed to April 21,1947 which was the actual date when General Clay ordered the DP camps closed to further admissions.

I also call your attention to the fact that the housing and employment provisions in the Act require revision. Nothing more should be required of the DPs admitted under the Act than is required for regular immigrants entering under the regular immigration laws. The present requirements are such as to make the Act extremely difficult if not impossible, of administration.

Since I feel that these matters have been already submitted to you, I merely call your attention to them in this brief way.

I wish to have you know, however, that it is the general opinion of all those interested in the subject with whom I have come in contact that the Act as passed is discriminatory and inadequate. I sincerely hope that you will reconsider the entire matter, and I shall greatly appreciate hearing from you.

Very truly yours,
Charles L. Aarons

Not only was the cutoff date a problem for the remaining refugees who were being persecuted in their country, but the limitations set by the immigration laws of the day were also an impediment in allowing DPs entry. Judge Aarons wrote the following letter to Wisconsin Senator Joseph McCarthy:

April 4, 1947
Sen. Joseph R. McCarthy
United States Senator for the State of Wisconsin
Senate Office Building
Washington 25, D.C.

Dear Senator:

This is one of the very rare occasions upon which I write to a United States senator but the occasion is so exceptional and the situation so urgent that I should not hesitate to communicate with you.

Without attempting to discuss the details, with which you are probably quite familiar, I express the hope that you will actively support the temporary liberalization of our immigration laws so as to permit a reasonable number of Displaced Persons to enter this country.

From all the information that I have obtained, these oppressed people, who are still suffering from the persecution of the war and pre-war years, will become an asset to our country if they are admitted. All this is beside the humanitarian considerations which demand that this country should take its fair share of such immigration. The delay which has already occurred has caused intense suffering.

In making this appeal to you I wish you to know also that I am writing this letter not only because of my own conviction of the necessity of immediate action but because of the many requests which have been made of me by a great many people who are representative of a variety of groups. I am in accord with these people that there is no greater duty incumbent upon us Americans today than to show that this country is willing to open its doors to persecuted but worthy people without regard to racial origin or religious affiliation.

Very truly yours,
Charles L. Aarons

Eventually, the planned 1945 cutoff date was abandoned, granting four hundred thousand displaced refugees of all faiths entry into the country between 1948 and 1953. Twenty percent of them were Jewish.

With the financial and emotional support of family or friends, they set-tled in ten different states, including Wisconsin, where the majority went to Milwaukee or Madison. In both cities, Jewish community leaders encouraged their arrival.

On January 17, 1946, the Jewish Welfare Fund was established in Wisconsin to help DPs and to raise money for a Jewish homeland. The situation of displaced war refugees inspired newfound enthusiasm for this cause. In a 1947 Gallup poll, 84 percent of American Jews and 82 percent of non-Jews answered "yes" when asked, "Do you support the establishment of the state of Israel?" In 1948, after the matter of the Jewish homeland was turned over to the United Nations, Jews finally received the slice of Palestine that would become the state of Israel.

Golda Meir (nee Mabowehz) spearheaded the Jewish Welfare Fund campaign in her adopted home state. By 1948, Wisconsin Jews had raised $2.1 million to assist victims of the war. It was not unusual to see a small blue-and-white tin box (*pushke*) in the homes of many Jewish fam-ilies throughout the country. Children and adults would regularly deposit their pennies, nickels, dimes, and quarters as a way of doing their part. Israel bonds were established with the hope that Israel would at last become a safe haven for Jews from all over the world. That hope became the glue that held American Jews, of all origins and religious practices, together as one.

In April 1950, the Resettlement Committee of Madison, chaired by Rabbi Manfred Swarsensky, organized a statewide conference on DPs. Arthur Greenleigh, executive director of United Service for New Amer-icans, had high praise for the organization's efforts. A *New Neighbors* pam-phlet printed by the Resettlement Committee quoted Greenleigh as saying that the work "demonstrated once more the community's un-swerving devotion to the enormous task American Jewry faces in making it possible for thousands of homeless Jews in camps in Europe to begin new lives in this country." Greenleigh hailed the conference as a "mag-nificent contribution to the DP program."

The Jewish Welfare Fund, the Wisconsin branch of the National Council for Jewish Women, and families from throughout the state reached out to the DPs to provide homes and jobs. Albert Beder, who spent time in the Dachau concentration camp during the war, was one such DP who received help from the Jewish Welfare Fund. By the time he was liberated, Beder had contracted typhoid fever and weighed just eighty pounds. After being nursed back to health in a hospital, he was placed in a DP camp in Europe. Mr. Beder recalls:

> Among the DPs were Jews, Poles, and others who had been in forced labor camps. Finally, I received a visa to go to America with the help of HIAS [Hebrew Immigrant Aid Society]. I traveled by ship to New York, where I had no relatives and spoke only German. By 1947, I met a peddler in night school who knew that there were some jobs in Appleton, Wisconsin. I ended up going there and being hired by Cohen Brothers Fruit Company. By then I had gained my weight and strength back and was able to lift heavy bags of fruits and vegetables onto trucks for sixty dollars a week. In October 1950 I was drafted into the army during the Korean War. Because I could speak German, I was sent back to Germany, where I ran a German youth center.

Beder was not bitter about being sent back to Germany. "A lot of Germans weren't really killers," he said, adding, "I ended up without hate. If you carry hate, you only hurt yourself." At age eighty-five, Beder lived in a comfortable house with his wife, Ruth, in a suburb of Milwaukee, where he has spoken about the Holocaust to schoolchildren and church groups. Beder explained that he chose to share his story "to speak for those who cannot speak, those whose voices were taken away."

THE RISE AND FALL OF
SMALL-TOWN JEWISH COMMUNITIES

Life is like riding a bicycle. To keep your balance,
you must keep moving.
—Albert Einstein

The postwar era of prosperity in Wisconsin and throughout the nation from 1945 to 1964 resulted in a skyrocketing national birth rate, later referred to as the Baby Boom. With more disposable income, families built new homes and formed new neighborhoods in the suburbs. Small towns of Wisconsin flourished, and Jewish communities prospered with new homes, synagogues, and successful businesses in those areas throughout the 1940s.

However, these same Jewish communities began to decline in the 1950s, '60s, and '70s as larger cities and higher education beckoned the next generation. As the postwar period gave rise to the GI Bill, which granted World War II veterans money to further their education, college enrollment among Jews soared. By 1964, 80 percent of Wisconsin's young Jewish people attended a four-year college, usually in locations far away from their rural communities.

The pursuit of higher education was not the only factor that led to the Jewish vacuum in most of small-town Wisconsin. As shopping trends veered toward the large malls of the 1950s and beyond, many small family-owned Jewish businesses could not survive.

Those who grew up in Viroqua speak fondly of Felix's General Store, where the townspeople could buy anything from boys' undershirts to kitchen dish towels. Started in 1905 by Russian immigrant Max Felix, the store thrived for decades as Max's son Rollie and later his grandson Steve joined him in business. Felix's General Store later changed its name to Felix's Men's and Women's Wear in the 1980s. However, the more modern focus was not enough to keep the store in step with the wave of the future. In 2000, Felix's closed its doors after it could no longer compete with the larger retail chains that had begun to appear in small-town malls. In Sheboygan, Hoffman's Flowerland survived as the last Jewish-owned shop in the city.

Despite the demise of many family-owned establishments, some Jewish businesses that began in rural communities grew to become successful statewide or even nationwide companies. The five-hundred-seat Campus Theatre, started by Ben Marcus in Ripon, grew into the Milwaukee-based Marcus Corporation, a major network of hotels, restaurants, and theaters that dot the state. Lewis E. Phillips set up shop in Eau Claire to sell his newly invented cookware device called a pressure cooker. His small business blossomed to become a major corporation known throughout the country as National Presto Industries, Inc. Eau Claire's Memorial Public Library, the planetarium within the Science Hall of the University of Wisconsin–Eau Claire, and the Eau Claire Senior Center bear the Phillips name in testimony to his philanthropic desire to give back to the city that provided him with so much opportunity.

Although many businesses successfully flourished beyond their small-town beginnings, by the late 1900s little remained of the Jewish communities in cities such as Stevens Point. The white clapboard building that was Beth Israel Congregation is all that remains of the once-thriving Jewish community. In the 1980s, when the congregation no longer had enough members to form a minyan, the building was deeded to the Portage County Historical Society. Now it houses a museum that serves as a reminder of the once vital Jewish presence in the city.

By 1965, the Moses Monifiore membership in Appleton had voted to join the United Synagogues of America, which officially made it a part of the Jewish Conservative movement. This change made it possible for men and women to sit together during religious services and gave greater recognition to the important roles that women had always played in the health of the congregation as they held fund raising events and reached out to the greater community through charitable deeds. As another sign of modernization, the yearly records that had been written in Yiddish were translated into English. On June 14, 1970, a new modern building on the city's developing northeast side was proudly dedicated. Although its name remained the same, the distinct shift in its congregants' needs over the years attracted new members and the promise of future growth. However, the Jewish community of Appleton, once the second largest in the state, was not immune to the demographic shifts of the latter 1900s. Before long the membership of the new congregation began to slip away, necessitating a move to a smaller facility and the employment of a part-time rabbi for the small number of Jews who stayed.

In Sheboygan, once home to three Orthodox synagogues at the peak of Wisconsin's Jewish diaspora, only Congregation Beth El has remained. The membership of the once crowded Conservative synagogue has become too small to retain a rabbi. Instead, two laypeople from the congregation started to conduct weekly services. "We're just trying to hang on," resident Harold Holman said. In spite of that sense of loss, he is clear about his continuing fondness for the city. "I'm very proud of Sheboygan. I've had a good life here." Although he still enjoys living in his hometown, he regrets having watched the Jewish community shrink down to approximately thirty families. "It's a sad story," he said. "It all fell apart when the kids left and never came back."

Holman is not alone in his affection for the city. More than three hundred Jewish former residents returned to Sheboygan for a reunion in

August 1999. Holman, who was a co-chair of the event, recalled, "They flocked here from all over the United States, France, and Israel." They were there to reminisce, to exchange tales about growing up together, and to pay homage to a place where they thrived, establishing successful businesses and becoming part of the secular community where they felt safe and welcomed. Perhaps David Schoenkin, whose grandfather Charles settled in Sheboygan as a scrap iron peddler, best summed it up when he told the *Sheboygan Press*, "Wisconsin opened its arms to those who wanted to build new lives and have the freedom to practice their religion."

Not every small-town Jewish congregation suffered closure due to twentieth-century changes, however. The Sons of Abraham Congregation in La Crosse has kept its doors open to serve approximately 125 congregants. Although by 1948 its members had enough financial stability to build a formal Orthodox synagogue, it could not sustain itself by the later 1900s. By 1992 it morphed into a Conservative congregation under the guidance of Rabbi Simcha Prombaum. Slowly its membership numbers climbed as the congregation drew religious Jews from the surrounding areas of Viroqua, Tomah, and parts of southeastern Minnesota, where Jewish communities lacked enough people to have their own synagogues.

Following suit, Wausau's Mt. Sinai Reform Temple meets the religious needs of Jews from that city and the surrounding towns of Stevens Point and Marshfield. And Green Bay's Congregation Cnesses Israel remains an active force in that community.

On September 21, 1953, the Jewish community of Green Bay celebrated the fiftieth anniversary of the congregation's existence. At the ceremony, these words were spoken about the first few Jewish families in Green Bay:

> The little group grew and flourished. Somehow they found their way to these two little northern communities of Green Bay and Fort Howard. John Baum came here from Boston, where he had fled from Russian Poland. William Sauber, a candy salesman, thirsted for intellectual companionship in the long lamp-lit evening and found it with Azriel Kanter and others who gathered at the Kanter home on Madison and Lake streets. Here then were the roots of a Jewish community. Above all else, they felt the need for prayer, for solace, for faith in their Creator to

whom all Jews had turned throughout the ages. Soberly on each
Friday afternoon they left their arduous tasks of the week,
arrayed themselves in their very best, and prepared to welcome
the Sabbath. Fortunately, in Azriel Kanter, they had a spiritual
leader. He was teacher, *shochet*, chazen [cantor] and mohel [one
who performs ceremonial circumcisions] combined and served
the others in these various capacities. His home became the spiritual meeting place for the little group. . . . September 15, 1889,
there was filed in the Office of Register of Deeds for Brown
County formal Articles of Organization for Congregation
Cnesses Israel of Green Bay, Wisconsin. The incorporators were
listed as Isaac Cohen, William Sauber, and Rev. Azriel Kanter. . . . Sunday, September 4, 1904, just six days before Rosh
Hashanah, was the great day—the opening of the shule of their
own. William Sauber and B. Bronstein had the honor of carrying the two scrolls of Holy Writ from the basement. Each
member in turn proudly ascended the altar steps and stood
attentively while Azriel Kanter read a portion from the Torah.

Far from the ideas of its earliest founders, Congregation Cnesses has
added a twenty-first-century twist to its Conservative form of Judaism—
a woman rabbi, Rabbi Shaina Bacharach, joins ranks with Dena Feingold, who grew up in Janesville and became the first woman rabbi in the
state in 1985. Rabbi Feingold went on to preside as the spiritual leader
of the Beth Hillel Reform Temple in Kenosha.

Rabbi Feingold recalls her family's efforts to maintain Jewish practices while she was growing up in Janesville as the only Jewish girl her age
in the town. "Being in a community where there are not many Jews
forces you to consider your own religious identity," Feingold said. Her
family made sure that as well as being very involved in the interfaith
community, she and her siblings received exposure to their religious roots
by traveling to the closest Jewish congregation for both Hebrew school
and religious holiday services.

Although the Jewish life in small-town Wisconsin has become only a
footnote in the Jewish history of the state, many people who grew up and
flourished in such communities look back with the fondest of memories.
Barbara Garber Essock, who spent her childhood in Wisconsin Rapids,

later recalled, "I had wonderful memories growing up in the Rapids and look back on my life as one of many more good times than bad—and always filled with love and security."

THE POSTWAR BOOM IN
MILWAUKEE AND MADISON

A righteous man falls down seven times and gets up.
—King Solomon, *proverbs 24:16*

In contrast to the dwindling Jewish communities in small towns, Milwaukee and Madison maintained the largest Jewish populations in the state in the second half of the twentieth century. To accommodate the religious needs of the Madison community, two new religious buildings were erected to replace three smaller synagogues that included Beth Jacob, Adas Jeshurun, and Agudas Achim. In 1950, the Agudas Achim congregation changed both its name and its building to become Beth Israel Center. Twelve years later, Adas Jeshrun closed its doors to join forces with the new congregation. Although Beth Israel was considered less Orthodox than any of its predecessors, it did not officially join the Conservative movement until the late 1960s. As the first Conservative synagogue in Madison, it added yet another stratum of Jewish worship to the community. Congregants who sought out religious observance that fell somewhere in between the rigorous adherence to Orthodox traditional practices and the more modern approach of the Reform temples found their place there. Temple Beth El, which was founded in 1939, dedicated its new building the same year with a Reform service that included the singing of "Ayn Kelahaynu" (No one like our Lord) and "America the Beautiful." These song choices reflected the congregants' devotion to the Jewish faith combined with a desire to assimilate to the new world in which they were living.

As an example of the interfaith fellowship that existed, Rev. Alfred W. Swan of Madison's First Congregational Church expressed the growing respect for Wisconsin's Jewish population when speaking at Temple Beth El's dedication: "To the Synagogue the world is forever indebted for the origin and inspiration of the Word of God. . . . May the days of our years and yours find us together in unbroken fellowship as citizens in our fair and fortunate land."

During the 1950s, the city of Milwaukee maintained varied congregations where Jews could express their religious faith in whatever way they chose, be it Orthodox, Conservative, or Reform. However, Rabbi Louis Switchkow, who led the Conservative congregation Beth El Ner Tamid and coauthored the book *A History of Jews in Milwaukee* in 1963, opined that Orthodoxy in the postwar period was "a very tenuous affair." In later years, in fact, the choices broadened in both Madison and Milwaukee to include Hassidic, Orthodox, Conservative, Reconstructionist, and Humanist groups.

By 1951, physicians, lawyers, and successful businessmen had replaced the Jewish peddlers of days gone by. Although Jews made up only 3 percent of Milwaukee's population, 20 percent of the doctors and 17 percent of the attorneys in the city were Jewish. Jews also provided significant contributions to other industries. The needlework trade of yesteryear was transformed into nationally known clothing lines such as Florence Eiseman children's clothes and Jack Winter designs. Kohl's corner grocery store in suburban Milwaukee's Bay View became Wisconsin's largest grocery store chain, and Aaron Scheinfeld and Elmer Winter founded Manpower, which provided millions of offices with temporary help. Harry Soref and Samuel Stahl developed a laminated padlock that has become internationally known as Master Lock, while Max H. Karl founded the Mortgage Guarantee Insurance Company (MGIC), the largest private mortgage insurer in the world.

As the Jewish community prospered, its members never forgot those less fortunate in their midst. The recent war had left plenty of reminders of those needing help in its wake. They were the soldiers who returned home with prosthetic hooks for hands and the shell-shocked who struggled with memories that could not easily be shaken. To meet their needs, the Jewish community of Milwaukee called upon the Jewish Vocational Service, first established in 1938 to help people who had lost their jobs during the Great Depression. In the postwar period this organization ramped up to help the wounded retrain and adjust to life with new disabilities. It was the first rehabilitation agency in the United States and by 1980 had become the largest in the nation outside of New York City. Its staff, which grew to include six hundred people, served not only veterans of the war but also the elderly, war refugees, and welfare recipients.

In addition, Milwaukee's Jews who had been able to flee Germany before the war began had established the New Home Club to help themselves adjust to their lives in Milwaukee. The organization was infused with a fresh vitality as Jewish survivors of the Holocaust joined their predecessors. Like the many organizations that originated in the 1800s, the New Home Club offered civics and English classes to the latest group, who had lost so much and needed to start anew.

Many DPs were employed through their Jewish neighbors or relatives. Some, like immigrant generations who had come before them, eventually developed businesses on their own. Harri Hoffmann, who escaped Kristallnacht, founded Hoffco Shoe Polish Company in the late 1940s, after selling the polish from door to door that his wife, Herta, concocted in their kitchen. The Harri Hoffmann Company remains in operation on Milwaukee's North Water Street as a symbol of the vital manufacturing entrepreneurship of the past.

Alfred Bader, who at age fourteen fled Austria via the *Kindertransport* in 1938, was interned in a Canadian camp with other European refugees suspected of being "alien enemies." Such fenced-in encampments were scattered throughout the United States and Canada until after the war was over. Upon his release Bader studied chemical engineering at Queen's University and Harvard. When he arrived in Milwaukee as a paint chemist, he cofounded the Aldrich Chemical Company in 1951. It eventually became the largest supplier of organic paint in the nation. As the list goes on, perhaps Joseph Peltz best articulated the can-do attitude that prevailed at the time. Having gone from a junk dealer to owner of a very successful recycling business, Peltz said in a 1956 interview, "There is no country like America. . . . If you have the spirit, nothing can stop you."

SPEAKING OUT AGAINST INJUSTICE

We do not know our own power to change and to effect change.
But we must act, that is in our power. We must do our part
and we have to hope that God is indeed attentive.
—Rabbi Baruch M. Bokser

The 1960s were turbulent times for African Americans, who were struggling to gain an unimpeded right to vote, to send their children to non-segregated schools, to have access to decent housing, and to be treated with the same respect as their white counterparts. As African Americans began to speak up for reforms under the leadership of Dr. Martin Luther King Jr., Jews throughout the country joined them at civil rights marches and demonstrations. In accordance with the principle of *tikkun olam* (a responsibility to repair the world), large numbers of Wisconsin Jews boarded buses and planes to the south, joining activists known as "Freedom Riders" from all over the country to express their commitment to civil rights.

Rabbi Richard Winograd of the University of Wisconsin's Hillel headed for Birmingham, Alabama, on May 7, 1963, with eighteen other Conservative rabbis. They had just attended a Rabbinical Assembly Convention of four hundred rabbis in New York at which the plight of southern African Americans was on the agenda. With the lingering memories of those who witnessed the Holocaust in silence and did nothing, the rabbis resolved that they must speak out against the injustices that were taking place in the south. They quickly passed the Birmingham Resolution, contributed funds, and sent nineteen volunteers from the convention to join Dr. King in the civil rights struggle. News reports had already warned the group of the volatile conditions that existed in Birmingham, including the animosity met by other Jewish leaders. Two rabbis had already been jailed for participating as Freedom Riders. Nevertheless, upon their arrival in Birmingham, Winograd and his fellow travelers registered at the all–African American G. S. Gaston Motel, defying the city's Jim Crow laws of the time.

During the August 26, 1963, March on Washington, the president of the American Jewish Congress, Joachim Prinz, spoke from a podium at the Lincoln Memorial, explaining why many Jews had joined the civil rights movement:

> As Jews we bring to this great demonstration in which thousands of us proudly participate, a two-fold experience—one of the spirit and one of the history—a sense of complete identification and solidarity born of our own historic experience.

Two years later, Edgar Feige, a young assistant professor of economics at the University of Wisconsin–Madison, climbed aboard a bus with a group of Jewish students from Hillel. They felt it was their duty to show support for southern African Americans in their struggles. On March 25, 1965, the bus from Madison headed for Alabama to join Dr. King in a march from Montgomery to Selma, in support of the 1965 Voting Rights Act that was about to be voted on in Congress.

Upon arrival, Feige and the UW students marched in tandem with local residents and other activists who dared to put their lives on the line. "Elderly bystanders watched from their front porches with tears streaming down their cheeks," Feige recalled. A young University of Wisconsin woman left the line of marchers to take an older African American man by the arm, in what was meant to be a friendly gesture, urging him to join the group on the street. He pulled back. "If I were ever caught touching a white woman, I'd be a dead man," Feige remembers him saying. "Joining the march was a frightening experience," Feige admitted, especially after news got out that the Ku Klux Klan had killed a participant in the march from one of the buses that day. However, he remembers that his dedication to the cause grew stronger than ever, despite the risk. "I had always thought that commitment led to action," he reflected, "but that day I realized that action itself can lead to commitment."

During the time of protests in the south Father James Groppi, a Catholic priest from Milwaukee, was leading the fight in Wisconsin. The son of poor Italian immigrants, Father Groppi sympathized with the plight of African Americans. Groppi led frequent marches and demonstrations in the streets of Milwaukee's all-white south side, advocating for open housing in the city. When riots broke out, leading to the priest's several arrests, Milwaukee's Jewish B'nai B'rith organization was one of the few white groups to openly support him. B'nai B'rith proposed a human rights award to honor Groppi. A February 27, 1968, article in the *Mil-waukee Sentinel* reported that, despite petitions in opposition to the award, fifty council delegates of the B'nai B'rith organization voted unanimously in favor of it.

Several Milwaukee Jewish leaders joined Groppi in his efforts. Dr. Jay Larkey, a retired obstetrician and gynecologist, recalls those times vividly. "As a little boy I grew up at 27 Fifty-Third Street, where the deed to our house [had once] read, no Jews or Negroes allowed. . . . In the 1920s, everything west of Sixtieth Street in Milwaukee was restricted," he explained. "Since then, I've always felt that I didn't want to deny any other people their due right to live where they wanted. . . . When I began the march over the Sixteenth Street viaduct with Reverend James Groppi, it became the longest bridge in the world—a link between Africa and Poland."

When marchers began to be stoned by jeering crowds or gassed by the police, Larkey felt that he could do the most good as a physician if he helped the wounded rather than take part in the marches. With that mission in mind, he set up a temporary emergency room at St. Boniface Hospital, where he cared for the injured.

Larkey later used his influence at the hospital to make sure that an African American physician was hired on staff. Dr. Bill Finleyson soon became one of the first practicing African American physicians in a Milwaukee hospital. He and Larkey remain good friends, participating in a task force on African American–Jewish relations together.

On June 13, 1972, the Milwaukee chapter of B'nai B'rith honored Dr. Larkey with its annual Human Rights Award, recognizing his "activity and personal commitment toward the goal of better understanding among the various religious, racial, or ethnic groups in our community."

OTHER BATTLES OF THE SIXTIES

How sad. How bitter that the sons of our liberators
should now be the ones to do something like this.
—Survivor of Bergen-Belsen concentration camp,
speaking of the My Lai massacre

While the civil rights movement was under way, the country was also embroiled in the Vietnam War halfway across the world. Once again, Jewish youth joined others in great numbers to protest what they considered to be the wrong course for the United States. In the late 1960s the University of Wisconsin–Madison, along with University of California–Berkeley, became the site of the most active, and at times the stormiest, campus demonstrations in the country. Paul Soglin, who became Madison's first Jewish and youngest mayor in 1973, played a strong leadership role in speaking out against the war while a student on campus. Soglin estimated that about 20 to 30 percent of student participants in the antiwar movement were Jewish.

Students were not alone in their protest of the war. Jewish UW professors Ted Finman and Maurice Zeitlin joined with Jewish and non-Jewish faculty to found the organization Professors for Peace. Both faculty and students were willing to face rounds of tear gas and the threat of arrest to speak out against a war that was costing thousands of American and Vietnamese lives with no positive end in sight.

The Vietnam War was not the only battle that concerned Jews in the sixties. On June 5, 1967, the Six-Day War broke out in the Middle East when Egypt, Jordan, Lebanon, and Syria attacked the new nation of Israel. Milwaukee's Jewish leaders again rallied to raise funds for the Jewish homeland that they had helped to establish. With dedication and effort, the Jewish Welfare Fund raised $1.7 million in less than a month. The money was used to help repair the damage left by the struggle in which Israel remained standing as a haven for the Jewish people.

A SHOUT-OUT TO FREE RUSSIAN JEWRY

We shall protest—we shall march—and we shall overcome.
—Morris B. Abram, president of the American Jewish
Committee, at conference on Soviet Jewry, 1965

On another front, the Jewish population was struggling in the post-Stalin Soviet Union. Although the harsh treatment of Jews was loosened a bit under Leonid Brezhnev's hand, religious oppression, professional and educational restrictions, and strong anti-Semitism were still present in the 1960s. Many Jews petitioned to get out of the country, but their requests were rejected time after time, leading them to become known as "refuseniks." Those who applied for an exit visa did so at great personal risk since they could have lost their jobs or suffered other penalties for having "betrayed" their country.

In the decades between the 1960s and 1980s, Jews from New York to California rallied to "free Soviet Jewry." The US government took note and began to apply pressure for the release of individuals who had applied to leave the Soviet Union. Such weight helped to open the door just a crack, allowing a relatively small number of Jewish refugees out from behind the Iron Curtain to settle in the United States.

The Smuglin family was among the Russian immigrants who ended up in Wisconsin. As physicians in Moscow, Claudia and Mark Smuglin had a nice apartment by Russian standards. However, despite their relative financial comfort, they could feel anti-Semitism closing in on them. Their eldest son, Leonid, sensed it, too. "I felt suffocated, almost claustrophobic," Leonid recalled. "I was issued a passport at age sixteen. But, under the words 'ethnic national origin' was stamped the word JEW." That was code for not being allowed to leave the Soviet Union, a privilege that his friends at school had. Although elderly people were allowed to attend Jewish religious services, young people were strongly discouraged from doing so. "If someone my age tried to enter a synagogue, there would be the KGB [Soviet Secret Service] and police across the street with cameras. One might be expelled from school on some trumped-up charges if identified," Leonid explained. "It was completely intimidating."

In 1974, the US Congress passed an amendment to the Jackson-Vanik Trade Reform Act. In exchange for favored trade status with the United States, the Soviet Union's emigration policies toward Jews were supposed to become more lenient. In practice, it meant that a certain number of Jews would be allowed to leave the Soviet Union. "It was my window of opportunity," Leonid said. When he applied to travel to America, the KGB came to question his parents, suggesting that they should have their son examined by a psychiatrist. His mother, a neurologist, persuaded the authorities that her son was of sound mind. After much paperwork and eight months of scrutiny by the authorities, Leonid was allowed to leave his place of birth in 1976. With his parents' blessings, he ventured alone to Green Bay, Wisconsin, at age seventeen. A close friend of his mother's who had emigrated from Moscow to Wisconsin decades before had agreed to serve as his sponsor. "I was so lonely," Leonid said of his first months in Wisconsin. "I thought I knew some English, but I quickly found out that I couldn't speak it at all. I felt very isolated." He also recalled how overwhelmingly big everything appeared, from cars to grocery stores and shopping malls. After working as a dishwasher in a small restaurant and obtaining his Wisconsin residency, Leonid enrolled in the University of Wisconsin a year later.

In the meantime, his parents and younger brother, Ilya, were preparing to join him. After obtaining the mandatory permission needed from their elderly parents and agreeing to hand over their apartment to a member of the Russian police—free of charge—they arrived three years later, in 1979. Their host family, who volunteered with the Madison Jewish Social Services to help them get started on their lives in Wisconsin, greeted them at the Dane County Regional Airport.

In spite of having to leave loved ones and all their financial possessions behind, the Smuglin family considers themselves lucky to have left when they did. For the next eight years, from 1980 to 1988, very few Jews wishing to leave the Soviet Union were granted exit visas. The refuseniks who applied to leave during those years not only risked losing their jobs, but their phones were often tapped and they were watched carefully. "They were stuck in a country that didn't want them," Leonid said.

A NEW WAVE OF RUSSIAN IMMIGRANTS

A few hours ago I was almost a slave in Moscow. Now I am a free
woman in my own country. It is the moment of my life.
—Ida Nudel, former refusenik from the Soviet Union, 1987

Because the situation remained difficult for Soviet Jews throughout the
1980s, the pressure from Jewish communities in the United States and
other countries, including Israel, became stronger. On a chilly morning
in December 1987, young and elderly Jews from all over Wisconsin piled
onto buses that drove all night to participate in the Freedom Sunday
Rally in Washington, DC. It was the largest Jewish demonstration ever
organized in the nation's capital. Three busloads of Jewish demonstra-
tors departed from Madison as a chartered plane took off from Milwaukee's airport to join the estimated crowd of two hundred thousand
people who came to support Soviet Jews. Collective voices chanted "Let
our people go" while Jewish dignitaries spoke from the podium. Perhaps
their voices were heard.

As the precarious Cold War period between the United States and
the Soviet Union began to thaw in the late 1980s, Soviet leader Mikhail
Gorbachev's policy of glasnost (openness) began to loosen exit restrictions. However, it was not until the final collapse of the Soviet Union in
1991 that the gates opened to Soviet Jews who felt like they had been held
captive for decades.

Unlike the scramble to accommodate the first wave of Russian
immigrants in the 1880s, this time, with the help of the Hebrew Immigrant Aid Society, the city of Milwaukee was ready to respond. Milwaukee philanthropists Marty Stein, Max H. Karl, and Ben Marcus led the
way as the Milwaukee Jewish Federation joined the United Jewish
Appeal to launch the Operation Exodus campaign. The local goal was
to raise $5.2 million for resettlement of Soviet Jews to Israel. Another
$1.8 million was to be used to aid domestic resettlement in the United
States. In the early 1990s, Milwaukee received three separate groups of
four hundred Jews from the Soviet Union. The number grew to nearly
three thousand by the end of the decade.

Although most of the Russian Jewish refugees settled in Milwaukee,
others came to Madison, where Jewish Social Services recruited eager

host families to greet the new arrivals; set up living accommodations; and donate furniture, food, and other immediate necessities of life. At the Dane County Airport, handshakes, smiles, and a few mutually understood words were exchanged between those whose ancestors had made the journey a century before and those whose relatives had chosen to stay behind. Their predecessors' choices had left a cultural chasm that would take time to narrow. Nevertheless, lasting friendships often arose between host families and the new arrivals, who found jobs, went back to school for retraining, learned to speak English, and quickly became self-sufficient contributors to the Wisconsin community.

THE ESSENTIALS: HUMOR, MUSIC, AND THE ARTS

Humor is just another defense against the universe. Look at the Jewish history. Unrelieved lamenting would be intolerable. So, for every ten Jews beating their breast, God designated one to be crazy and amuse the breast-beaters.
—Mel Brooks, comedian and writer

No account of Jewish life in Wisconsin or elsewhere would be complete without including the essential role that humor, music, and the arts have played in Jewish existence. As Jewish immigrants struggled against prejudice and poor living conditions, humor often provided comfort. From the 1880s through the 1930s, Jewish vaudeville comedians entertained audiences with song, dance, and self-effacing tales of the human condition that helped people laugh rather than cry. For example, one vaudeville comedian shared a shortened version of the Passover seder, which typically involves a lengthy reading of the exodus story from the Haggadah before the meal: "They tried to kill us, we survived, let's eat."

The comedians included Myron Cohen, Jack Benny, George Burns, Eddie Cantor, Sid Caesar, Fanny Brice, Groucho Marx, Milton Berle, and many others. Some of these later carried their vaudeville acts to the Borscht Belt, a group of resorts in the Catskill Mountains of New York, which attracted mostly Jewish audiences from the 1930s through the mid-1960s. As black-and-white televisions entered people's living rooms, Jews and non-Jews all over the country became familiar with a Jewish style of humor that lives on today in comedians such as Jackie Mason, who was born in Sheboygan as the son of a cantor. Mason also began his career as a cantor but realized that his calling lay in the world of comedy. He continues to perform his parables on Jewish life for audiences throughout the country.

Whether comedic or serious, Jews have also played a tremendous role in every aspect of filmmaking, from the development of the largest movie studios to writing, directing, producing, and acting. Carl Laemmle, who lived in Oshkosh and Milwaukee during the early 1900s, joined a long list of Jewish movie moguls as the founder of Universal Studios. The films turned out for the silver screen in those days often reflected the American culture that the one-time immigrants so thoroughly embraced.

Growing up in Milwaukee, Gene Wilder (born Jerome Silberman in 1933) turned his habit of trying to make his ailing mother laugh into a life-long passion for performing. He was probably best known to children of the 1970s as the actor who starred in the movie *Willy Wonka and the Chocolate Factory*, based on a book by Roald Dahl. However, both young and old will remember him in Mel Brooks's zany productions of *The Producers*, *Blazing Saddles*, and *Young Frankenstein*.

Milwaukee brothers Jerry and David Zucker, along with their high school friend Jim Abrahams, also seemed to inherit the desire to make people laugh. The three graduates of Milwaukee's South Shore High School collaborated to write, produce, and direct such spoof films as *Kentucky Fried Movie*, *Airplane*, and the *Naked Gun* series.

As important as humor and filmmaking are to the Jewish soul, so too is music. As soon as it was possible to afford music lessons, many Jewish immigrant families saw to it that their children were trained to play a musical instrument. From the earliest chants of the Hebrew prayers to the cantor's soulful tones of *Kol Nidre* on Yom Kippur, music has been an essential part of Jewish religious services and life events. Joyous celebrations, such as weddings, most often include the hora, a spirited circle dance accompanied by klezmer music first played by the Ashkenazi Jews of eastern Europe.

Ben Sidran, Wisconsin's renowned jazz pianist, composer, and author, has studied the interconnectedness between the Jewish experience and American music. Sidran pointed to the fact that the first clarinet strains of Jewish composer George Gershwin's "Rhapsody in Blue" echo the Semitic tones of Yiddish klezmer. Sidran has also documented

American influences on Jewish songwriters such as Albert and Harry Von Tilzer (born Gumbinsky), who wrote "Take Me Out to the Ballgame," and Irving Berlin (born Israel Baline), who composed quintessential American songs including "White Christmas," "God Bless America," and "This Is the Army, Mr. Jones."

Sidran, who was born in Racine, has contributed to the American music scene himself. He has performed with famed musicians Boz Scaggs and Steve Miller and played in recording sessions for Eric Clapton, the Rolling Stones, Peter Frampton, and Charlie Watts. Jazz fans may remember his contributions to the award-winning programs *Jazz Alive* and *Sidran on Record* on National Public Radio. In his book *There Was a Fire: Jews, Music and the American Dream*, Sidran summed up the place of music in Jewish life: "Since the beginning of the diaspora, Jews have taken folk songs and popular tunes from whatever country they happened to be passing through and embedded Hebrew prayers and sentiments in them. It appears that the sacred text is quite easily conveyed in popular song; or alternatively that any song becomes sacred when the community sings it for a higher purpose."

Marc Chagall of Russia, whose paintings and stained glass murals appear in museums around the world, including the Milwaukee Jewish Museum, perhaps best exemplifies Jewish art in the minds of many. But Wisconsin has been home to several artists who gained national or international respect. Aaron Bohrod, born in 1907 to a Russian immigrant grocer, was perhaps the most widely recognized. His still-life paintings appeared on the covers of *Time* magazine, representing daily objects while providing artistic, sometimes satirical, illustrations of the American way of life. During World War II, Bohrod served as an artistic war correspondent for *Life* magazine in the European theater and later had the role of artist in residence at the University of Wisconsin–Madison. His fellow artists on the faculty included renowned Jewish printmaker Alfred Sessler of Milwaukee.

In another part of the state, potter Abe Cohn was honored with the Wisconsin Visual Artists Lifetime Achievement Award. In 1970, Cohn founded the Door County Potters Guild, where he taught aspiring artists. An appreciative student remembered him saying, "You have to feel your soul, find your vision, find that thing you're compelled to do and keep following that." Cohn took his own advice at the Potters Wheel in Fish Creek from 1955 until the time of his death in 2013.

A JEWISH AMERICAN DREAM COME TRUE

America has saved not only my body, but also my soul.
It has restored my faith in the promise of
life and in the goodness of people.
—Rabbi Manfred Swarsensky of Temple Beth El in Madison,
from his book *Intimates and Ultimates*

In 1955 both the Madison and Milwaukee campuses of the University of Wisconsin established departments of Hebrew and Semitic studies, followed by the George L. Mosse and Lawrence A. Weinstein Center for Jewish Studies on these campuses in 1991. The intellectual scholarship developed within these academic disciplines has created a deeper awareness among its students of Jewish history, culture, and language, instilling a more complete understanding of a people whose past has often been misinterpreted.

By the 1970s Jews had become an integral thread in the fabric of Wisconsin's society. In the state that has customarily welcomed them, they have been given the opportunity to flourish, to live free, peaceful, and prosperous lives. As a sign of acceptance, a 1971 Gallup poll named Milwaukee's Goldie Mabowehz, by then Israel's prime minister Golda Meir, the most widely admired woman of the year. The honor was again bestowed upon the former Milwaukee activist in 1973 and 1974.

Whether born in Wisconsin or adopting the state as home, the Jewish people have contributed vastly to the place where they have chosen to live. Throughout their history in the state they have left their mark in business, education, philanthropy, sports, politics, music, literature, the arts, law, and medicine. Contributions that have affected the world far beyond Wisconsin's boundaries include Dr. Howard Temin's groundbreaking research that unlocked valuable clues to the causes and treatment of cancer and other devastating diseases. Dr. Temin, who worked at the University of Wisconsin's McArdle Lab for Cancer Research until shortly before his death in 1994, was awarded a shared Nobel Prize in 1975.

The Waisman Center on the University of Wisconsin–Madison campus, which treats developmentally disabled children throughout the region, is named in tribute to Dr. Harry Waisman, a pioneer in the research connecting a hereditary accumulation of an amino acid, phenylalanine, with the debilitating disease phenylketonuria. His findings have been essential in preventing countless numbers of children from becoming mentally disabled. The impact of his work has been felt worldwide.

Making a tremendous impact close to home, Madison brothers Robert and Irwin Goodman joined other philanthropists in Wisconsin to greatly enhance the lives of young and old, rich and poor with their numerous charitable contributions. These included donating funds for the Goodman Jewish Community Campus outside of Madison. The 154-acre grounds now provide a more permanent home for Camp Shalom, which was founded by Ben and Evelyn Minkoff in 1954 for children ages four through eleven. Later, additional opportunities for older kids were created. Camp Shalom now serves approximately one thousand Jewish and non-Jewish young people, offering scholarships to those who cannot afford tuition. In addition, the Goodmans funded Madison's first public swimming pool, open for everyone to enjoy. Their generosity lives on through the Goodman Foundation, which continues to improve the lives of many.

Jews have also made an impact in sports, with two in particular helping to keep sports alive in Wisconsin. Herb Kohl not only served as the US senator from Wisconsin from 1989 to 2003, but he also helped to retain professional basketball in the state by purchasing the Milwaukee Bucks in 1985. Alan "Bud" Selig can be credited with bringing another professional sport to Wisconsin when he purchased a Seattle baseball team and brought it to Milwaukee. Thousands of fans flock every summer to watch the Milwaukee Brewers in action.

US Senator Russ Feingold represented Wisconsin from 1993 to 2011. He followed in the footsteps of Wisconsin-born politicians such as Wilbur Cohen, secretary of health, education and welfare in 1958, and Newton Minow, chairman of the Federal Communications Commission in 1960. Steve Kagan of Appleton joined him in 2006 when he was elected to represent the eighth district of the state in the US Congress. At the State Supreme Court, Judge Myron Gordon, born in Kenosha, served as associate justice from 1961 to 1967, followed by his appointment as federal judge for the Eastern District of Wisconsin. Shirley Abrahamson became the first woman to serve on the Wisconsin Supreme Court when she was appointed in 1976 and the court's first woman chief justice in 1996. She is also the court's longest-serving member.

Many more Jews—too numerous to name—have contributed greatly to the state of Wisconsin and beyond. These have included the many Jewish academicians of the universities and colleges who have shared their valuable talents, expertise, research, and educational contributions.

THE TIES THAT BIND

The Jews are my unconscious.
—Alfred Kazin, author of *New York Jew*

The ancient and most meaningful tenets of Judaism include a belief in one God; the obligation to act justly and to help those in need (*tzedakah*); a responsibility to pray (*tefillah*); and the requirement to repent for one's wrongdoing (*tshuvah*). These principles laid out in the Torah (the first five books of the Hebrew Bible) have remained constant. However, one would be hard put to define today's brand of Judaism as a single set of practices or beliefs. Instead, Jews have become a conglomeration of Orthodox, Conservative, Reform, Reconstructionist, and Humanist ideas, from which each Jewish person is free to choose. In addition, some agnostics and atheists consider themselves culturally Jewish, whether in terms of social values, taste in foods, humor, or common understanding of the past, if not religiously.

In the past few decades, a growing number of mixed marriages have decreased the population of Jewish-born children as the older generation dies out. In addition, as assimilation has led many Jews to identify as Americans first, some Jewish leaders have grown concerned that Judaism will eventually fade away entirely in this country. However, in spite of such religious fragmentation and divided allegiances, strong ties remain to perpetuate the Jewish spirit. No matter where Jewish immigrants and their descendants originated, no matter how they practice their faith, a sense of a common ancestry that dates back to ancient times binds them together. They possess a mutual awareness of having overcome tremendous hardships with dignity and pride. Their cultural nuances—reflected in literature, ethnic foods, and humor—serve as a reminder of their Jewish identity.

The practice of remembering a close relative on the anniversary of their death is still carried on in most practicing Jewish homes as families light a *yahrtzeit* candle, taking time to remember their loved one. The ritual of acknowledging a boy's or girl's coming of age with a ceremony of Bar or Bat Mitzvah lives on, often with festive celebrations, albeit toned down significantly in Wisconsin, reflecting Midwest sensibilities. Families gather from near and far to sit together at a seder table during Passover—a holiday that celebrates freedom from oppression, not just for the Jewish people but for others who still hunger to be free. The centerpiece of matzoh (unleavened bread), which is eaten over the course of a week, serves to represent the rapid flight of the Jews from the harsh edicts of the Egyptian pharaoh, leaving no time for the bread to rise.

Although it is considered a minor holiday in Jewish congregations, Hanukkah is observed in many homes with the lighting of the menorah candles for eight nights. This ritual is often accompanied by the preparation of sizzling potato latkes (pancakes) fried in oil—a recipe that has been passed down through the generations with little variation. Both the burning candles and cooking oil are symbolic of the small flask of fuel that was found after the desecration of the temple in Jerusalem at the hands of Syrian oppressors in 168 BCE. It has been said that the small quantity remarkably lasted for eight days, allowing it to keep burning until it could be replenished. Throughout the ages, Jewish congregations have placed a source of illumination over their altars. Known as the Eternal Light, it is there to signify God's presence.

Many less-traditional Jews who rarely attend religious services may be drawn to congregations for the High Holy Days—Rosh Hashanah and Yom Kippur. In the week between the two holidays, each individual is called upon to reflect on any wrongdoing they have committed in the past year so that they may personally atone for their transgressions. In temples or synagogues around the world, the same Hebrew chants, prayers, and sounds of the shofar (ram's horn) can be heard, as they have been throughout Jewish history.

Even the Yiddish newspaper, established as *The Forverts* in 1897 as a voice of the Jewish immigrant, remains a remnant of early Jewish life in America. Although it is now distributed primarily in English as *The Jewish Daily Forward*, with topics of current interest, it continues to serve as a reminder of the people who came before.

As Jews have embraced their life in Wisconsin, they have left their cultural mark in other ways. Yiddish words, Jewish foods, and Jewish humor have found their way into the Badger state, adding to the rich cultural mix that it has become. It would not be unusual to hear a Packers fan of any faith proclaim that they had to *schlep* up to the top bleachers of Lambeau Stadium. A good man may commonly be referred to as a *mensch*. And who in Dairy Land hasn't grabbed a bagel to *nosh* on the way to work?

In the words of Miranne Lubar, who helped establish the Jewish Historical Society and Jewish Museum in Milwaukee, "Without our cultural heritage we have nothing. . . . We must preserve it so the next generation will learn from the past."

Albert Beder

Albert Beder, Milwaukee resident, was a prisoner at the Dachau concentration camp and was sent back to Germany during the Korean War. Beder has shared the story of his experiences with Milwaukee churches and schools.

WHS Museum Object ID 1985.92

This sweater was worn by prisoner #1A944, Tadeusz Kowalczyk, at the Auschwitz concentration camp. In 1968, Kowalczyk became a full professor at the University of Wisconsin–Madison and became nationally known for his research on ulcers in swine.

Ghita Bessman

Leonard Bessman was awarded the Distinguished Service Cross, Silver Star, and Purple Heart for his bravery during World War II. His wife, Ghita, of Madison, has been a longtime leader in the Jewish community.

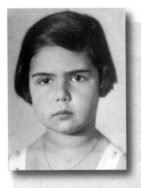

24, Elmscott Gardens,
Bush Hill,
London, N. 21.
England.

23rd July, 1939.

Mrs. Polgar,
4a, Quergasse,
Brünn,
Czecho-Slovakia.

My dear Mrs. Polgar,

      I have received your letter about Renate's
coming to England. I will arrange everything for her
with Mrs. Plaček and Mr. and Mrs. Daniels. You may
rest assured that I will do everything I possibly can,
- just the things I imagine you would do as her Mother.
These days must be terribly hard for you and you are
much in my thoughts, but you may be happy in the thought
that your little girl will be loved and cared for and
she will be received into Mr. and Mrs. Daniel's home just
as one of their own children. I trust this knowledge
will make these coming days a little less difficult for
you and your husband. I promise you both everything I
can do shall be done.

      Do write to me from time to time, I shall
always be delighted to hear from you.

      I shall be out of England from 28th July
until 25th August and am very glad Renate is coming
before I go and I can know that she is safely in her new
home.

      With every best wish and the assurance
        of my friendship,
          Yours sincerely,

            Grace M. Beaton.

Renata Laxova

Renata Laxova (nee Polgar) left on the last *Kindertransport* train to England at age
eight. A letter sent to the family of Renata Laxova's family detailed arrangements for
her transport to England and the family she would be living with.

WHi Image ID 72005

WHi Image ID 50058

Above: Newcomers to Milwaukee gather for a Passover seder after World War II. Passover commemorates the Jewish exodus out of Egypt. This seder in 1948 celebrated another exodus for the Jewish people.

Left: Helen Sinagub models the latest style of evening gown at a fashion show for the Council of Jewish Women in Madison, February 1948, as Lucille Martin and Alma Baron watch. Many Jewish women adopted American fashion.

Holocaust survivors Rose and
Bernard Katz made their way
to Oshkosh, Wisconsin, via
Goteborg, Sweden, in 1948.

WHi Image ID 56772

WHi Image ID 44872

The Katz family poses for a portrait on the day of their daughter Marilyn's 1973 Bat
Mitzvah at Temple B'nai Israel in Oshkosh. Girls did not have a Bat Mitzvah ceremony (the counterpart of a Bar Mitzvah) until the 1920s, when it was introduced with
the Reconstructionist movement.

Edward Deutschkron, son of Eva and Martin Deutschkron of Madison, watches his father light the menorah during Hanukkah of 1952.

WHi Image ID 56528

WHi Image ID 78877

Morris Heifitz, leader within the Conservative congregation Beth Israel in Madison, blows the shofar during Rosh Hashanah services. The shofar is blown on Rosh Hashanah, the first of ten days of repentance, in part to awaken Jews to examine their wrongdoings and repent.

WHi Image ID 81724

Holocaust survivor Alfred Hopf, once a prominent lawyer and banker in Germany, worked as a taxi driver upon arriving in Wisconsin.

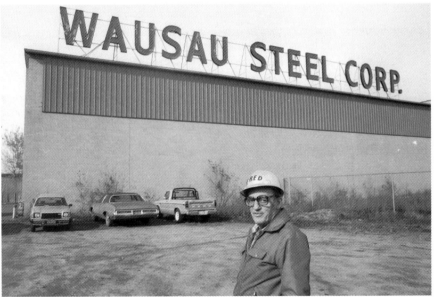

WHi Image ID 57108

Fred Platner escaped a German concentration camp in 1939, only to be recaptured by the Russians and sent to a Siberian labor camp the following year. After surviving the war, he relocated in 1951 to Wisconsin, where he rose to be vice president of Wausau Steel Corp.

WHi Image ID 23489

Rabbi Max Lipschitz of Beth Israel Center in Madison prepares a group of boys for their forthcoming Bar Mitzvahs in 1954.

Fred Moskol

A B'nai B'rith BBYO convention in Elkhart Lake in the mid-1950s. Young members of BBG and AZA gathered together for periodic conventions throughout the state.

WHi Image ID 106621

Robert and Irwin Goodman, generous philanthropists to the Jewish community and residents of Madison, with their mother, Belle Goodman, in 1960

Jewish Federation of Madison

Madison residents joined the Washington, DC, rally to free Soviet Jews in December 1987. It was the largest Jewish demonstration ever organized in the nation's capital.

LOUIS HELLER JOURNALS, 1948

The following are excerpts from a 1948 account written by Louis Heller about his family's emigration from Germany to Milwaukee in 1848. He details the efforts by his parents and later his siblings and himself as they worked to establish themselves in a trade in Milwaukee. As an adult, Louis Heller departed Milwaukee for Omaha, Nebraska, in search of work but returned after ten years, drawn back to the city that had been his family's first American home.

In 1848 Frederic the Great, king of Prussia, started a campaign to enlarge his country, causing a disturbance among the other provinces of which Bohemia, a province of Austria, was one. My parents [had a] very hard life, by being taxed by the government for every blade of grass they grew which was of use to them. Father and mother had been living a very close life and had saved up sufficient money for the emigration to America, having heard that there were innumerable opportunities for a happy life in this country. Bernard Heller and his wife, Sarah Levy Heller, lived in the little village of Czitau, about two hours from Prague. There were five children. Not needing passports at that time, they found it an easy matter to leave the country, having engaged a wagon and horses to take them to Hamburg, where they took passage on a sailing boat for New York. It was necessary for them to carry their own provisions for the ninety-day voyage to Milwaukee, provisions that included prunes, smoked fish, and smoked beef, the boat furnishing the bread and coffee. They disembarked at New York and engaged passage for Milwaukee, routed through the Erie Canal, work having been finished on that in 1825, which journey took them three weeks on the canal boat, that was hauled by horses and landing in Erie, Pennsylvania. From Erie they came by sailboat across the Great Lakes to Milwaukee, landing at the foot of Huron Street at a pier built of piles driven into the water that had planks lain across.

Can you imagine a husband and father landing in a strange country destitute and hungry with five children and twenty-five cents in his pocket? He left his family sitting on the pier, walked up Spring Street, and approached a stranger, asking if he could speak German, to advise him where to go to find work, which was imperative that he should have at once. He was referred to a party who immediately employed him at fifty cents a day using pick and shovel building a street. In the evening he found where he could employ his time working at his own trade, making sausage for a Mr. Hasselman, whose market was located on State Street between Fourth and Fifth in a cottage that still stands there. He found a shack for his family to live in that was located on what is now Seventh and Cherry streets. The shack was built against a bluff, one room with boxes for furniture. At the time the family moved in, Indians were camping on the bluff above them. Just one tepee of friendly Indians. The real work of the family started when they moved into the shack. Mr. Hasselman took kindly to Mr. Heller and took him with him to the slaughterhouses. He taught him how he could take the entrails of the cows and make liver sausage of them. Father took them home, chopped them with hand meat cleavers, Mother boiled the meat and helped make it into sausage. Then, early in the morning before going to his regular job, he went out to sell the sausages. It wasn't long before he had saved five dollars—a real saving in those days. With this five dollars, he started into business for himself. He walked out into the country and bought two calves which he brought back with him, carrying them when they got too tired to walk. He dressed and sold the calves and continued this as his regular business until he had saved up ten dollars. With that ten he bought a wagon and went to Mr. Schram, a banker, to borrow ten dollars to buy a horse and harness. Mr. Schram asked him what security he had and he answered, "Fifty thousand dollars: my wife, twenty-five thousand; and five children, each five thousand. Mr. Schram refused him, but he succeeded in getting it elsewhere. As time went on, equipped now with horse and wagon, it did not take long to accumulate the [tools] of hard labor. His earnings now were sufficient to safely buy him forty feet [of] frontage on Third Street and extending back to the Milwaukee River. There was a story and a half. . . . Mother was proud of the home and its comforts. There was a kitchen back of the market and living rooms upstairs. They had real beds to sleep in—a feather bed. Two more children had been born, the youngest, Louis, born August 22, 1852. Mother was a wonderful wife and mother, almost to an excess. She cooked, she cleaned, did the washing and ironing for the five children and had time to do mending and patching of clothes, besides being of great help to Father in the market. Her ambitions were to be a help to the needy and a leader in charity work, in which she was very much successful. She was on the organizers of Die Treue Schwestern, a society, which is still actively in existence.

Father had a restless disposition, caused by ambitions to be successful not only in his undertakings but for the future of his family. He strove hard in every direction. He was a very truthful man and respected by the community in which he lived, although we were the only Jews in that neighborhood.

The little frame house was becoming too small for the family to have creature comforts; he concluded that a larger house was necessary. And having twenty feet frontage he concluded to build a brick structure of three stories. In 1856, the family moved in. Sitting here now, we are looking at the settee that Mother ordered in 1856 for that very house. When the first floor was completed, a keg of beer was bought to celebrate. I remember running out of the old house early that morning, still in my nightgown, to put my head under the beer faucet and get the first drink of beer.

Father continued his trips in the country to buy livestock. The Jewish colony in the city continued to grow, compelling Father to add a kosher market. The frame house was occupied by my sister Caroline and her husband, who were set up in the grocery business by Father.

At the age of six I started in school. For about six months I attended the public school at Sixth and Juneau, in the very same building now occupied by the offices of the Pabst Brewing Company. [My parents] not being satisfied with the school, I was sent to a private school sponsored by the German element, to see that German was taught to their children. The school was run by Mr. Peter Engelman, who taught the higher studies—chemistry, algebra, geometry, French, English, and German were taught besides the regular ABCs, history, and arithmetic. A fine artist taught drawing, and singing was also included in the curriculum. School hours ran from 8:30 until 12:00 and from 1:00 until 3:00 for ten months of the year. Manners were particularly stressed. One of my strongest impressions of Mr. Engelman was having him tell us that whenever we passed an older person we must always tip our hats and greet them. Each morning as we came to school, Mr. Engelman stood on the walk, enjoying his morning pipe or cigar, greeted each of the children, and made inquiries about the welfare of our families. The big treat for the class was to go "botanizing" with Mr. Marine. We brought many specimens back for Mr. Engelman's collection, which is now over at the Milwaukee Museum.

We had a very large black Newfoundland dog, and my brothers, who were very fond of excitement, trained him to draw a sled. Father had given permission to them to make a harness for the dog and allowed them to go on excursions with their "dog team." One Sunday morning, when sledding was good, they hitched their dog for an excursion to Schlesinger's Villa, the Schlesingers' private home situated where the Milwaukee General Hospital now stands. They bundled me up and put me on the sled too so I might go along for the ride. We started off gaily, going full speed ahead, when suddenly Donau spied a dog who didn't quite meet his fancy. With a leap and bound, completely disregarding his precious load, he dashed for the dog, throwing me helter-skelter into the snow. At another time, [my] brothers planned an excursion to get some good apples, again at Schlesingers' Villa. This time they had a small wagon for the dog to pull. They started joyfully anticipating a feast. After locating a tree bearing the fruit they wanted, they were also located by the caretaker of the estate, who with a shotgun (whether or not it was loaded has never been answered) called to them to get out or he would shoot them. The dog was put into a trot to get away—all of them arriving home safely but minus apples and plus a good scare.

Albert, my eldest brother, was already working at learning a trade. Brother Adolph, four years younger and then about fourteen, was helping Father. In 1859 the gold rush to Pike's Peak in Colorado created some excitement in our home. Adolph, the second son, about sixteen years old, concluded that this was his opportunity to join the gold rush. After considering back and forth, my parents consented to let him go and bought a rifle and mold to make bullets. Evenings, when the regular [work] was finished, Adolph and I sat in front of a hot fire, melting lead to cast the bullets. Other matters coming up prevented him [from] joining the rush, and his musket and bullets became part of the home museum.

In the same year, my sister Sophia married in the new Temple B'ne Jeshurun that had been dedicated by Isaac Wise. Her husband, Phillip Goldsmith, also a Bohemian from Prague, was set up in the dry goods business in Chicago by my father. Not only was he able to start his son-in-law in business, but he had saved enough money to invest in ten acres of land on what is now Center Street between Fifth and Seventh. He paid thirty dollars an acre for land, which would now be worth about fourteen thousand dollars an acre. The original owner, after selling the land to my father, cut down and hauled away all the timber that had grown on that parcel of land.

The rumor that the Sioux Indians were again raiding the settlers in Manitowoc, Wisconsin, was started. There had been a massacre at New Ulm, Minnesota: so the farmers picked up their families and all their household goods they could load on their wagons and came to Milwaukee. I remember seeing a long line of wagons escorted down Third Street by the Grun Jaegers regiment, a volunteer regiment privately supported by the citizens of Milwaukee. The scare only lasted a few hours and the farmers started back again to their homes.

The Lincoln-Douglas campaign created a strained feeling in the North between the Republicans and Democrats. Both Lincoln and Douglas made speeches here in Milwaukee. I failed to hear either of the speeches, but I did see Douglas riding through the streets in a black carriage drawn by black horses, covered with black cotton blankets with gold lettering on them—"Vote for Douglas." My family were all staunch Republicans, and when the Civil War broke out, my brother Albert ran away and enlisted in Chicago. He was only nineteen years old but gave his age as twenty-one. His regiment was the Ellsworth Zouaves. The regiment went to Cairo, Illinois, pulled down the Confederate flag and raised the Stars and Stripes. Then came back to Chicago and their term of enlistment being over, they were discharged. Albert reenlisted for three years in the Federal Army. He was ordered to report to General Rosencrantz's division in Kentucky. From there he was transferred to the army under General Siegel's command. Among the many engagements in which he took an active part, we will only mention a few. From Kentucky they swung into Tennessee, taking possession of Nashville, engaged at Lookout Mountain, and many other battles along the march to Georgia. Then in '65 he was mustered out. He was a very fine draftsman. The general in command heard of his ability and asked him if he would like to join the topographical division of the army. He refused, saying that he did not want to leave the boys. My brother Adolph, on the Fourth of July of the year Albert returned, was having his own private celebration. Each year on that day there was a parade of militia and civic associations. Adolph had found a piece of gas pipe about ten inches long, plugged up one end, and filed a hole for touching it off; loading it with powder and added a pea for ammunition. He mounted a piece of wood and placed it in front of him on the sidewalk facing the road on which the parade was to travel. As the band approached, Adolph put a match to the powder and aimed so successfully that the explosion shot the pea into the leg of one of the musicians, disrupting the procession for a short time. The result was a lawsuit, and Father had to pay the doctor bill and loss of time. We all stood back in fear and trembling for fear the thing would explode. I ran away and Adolph got a good threshing for it. Upon Albert's return, he married a cousin of his, and Father set him up in a grocery business in Chicago.

During these years, I continued going to school. The games we played were very like those that boys and girls play now—hide-and-seek, cracking the whip, baseball, pompom pull away. I had the added pleasure of playing on the boats that were docked practically in our backyard. The companies were interested in having the boys, as they grew up and became sailors, so they were glad to have me come aboard and stimulate my interest in sailing. I was given the run of the boats, climbing all over the rigging, learning sailing terms and how a boat is handled. Many years later this knowledge I had gained was valuable to me in helping me with my hobby of building models of these boats.

In '67 I graduated from school. Mother was determined that I take part in the graduation exercises. . . . I was given the role of the grave digger in Hamlet. I thought I was entitled to a better part than that, but Mother was quite satisfied—knowing nothing about Hamlet.

In 1865 shortly after my brother was married, I was allowed to go to Chicago to visit him. I made the trip all by myself on the train. It took three and a half hours to get there. The train was pulled by a wood-burning locomotive—two cars and a baggage car. The cars were held together by links so that each car had to have its own brakeman to work the works of the brakes to prevent bumping. When the engineer blew his whistle twice, it was a signal for the brakeman to apply the brakes. The big city had very little appeal for me. After the excitement of the trip and the pleasure of seeing my brother again, I was ready to turn right back and come home again.

One morning, while busily working in the market helping Father, we suddenly heard a man running down the street and shouting frantically. When he got near the store, we heard, "Lincoln was assassinated last night!" Father dropped what he was doing and sat down and wept.

Everyone in our block was affected in the same way. They all idolized President Lincoln; so much that the citizens of Milwaukee concluded to have a mock funeral—a hearse with a coffin in it drawn by a team of black horses. Three prominent men walked on either side of the hearse as a cortege of honor. A long line of carriages and buggies followed.

My brother Adolph had been working for some time in Rockford, Illinois, learning the butcher trade. By the time I finished school, he came back to Milwaukee, married Bertha Frank, and Father set him up in the butcher business. As soon as I finished school, I went to work for him. I had to go live with him because I had to be at work by four o'clock in the morning. By six o'clock I had the four horses in my charge cleaned and fed. I earned fifteen dollars a month and room, board, and washing. I worked for him for two years. In '69 I went to Cincinnati to visit my sister who was living there. While there I got a job in a doll factory and stayed for two years. Upon returning to Milwaukee in '71 I again went to work for Adolph and stayed with him another two years.

In 1872 while on a picnic at the Pereles summer home, on the river, we were going boating. As Julia was about to step into the boat one of the boys shoved it away and she fell waist deep in the water. I was standing in back of her and quickly jumped in and pulled her out. That was my first meeting with the girl who later became my wife. She was fifteen and I was twenty. At a family picnic in Cedarburg we met again the same summer. On the picnic I got her permission to call on her and took advantage of it more and more often. After several months we became engaged. A serious rumor [said] that she was marrying me in gratitude for having saved her life by pulling her out of the water, but our fifty-two years of marriage proved quite otherwise. We rented a house on Astor Street and set up housekeeping there. We had to pay one hundred dollars a year rent. We were married on July 12 in Temple B'ne Jeshurun [1874] and returned to the Blacks' home on Reed Street for the wedding dinner.

Now things began happening that weren't so pleasant. My brother Adolph persuaded me to go into the glue manufacturing business with him and his father-in-law. He thought he saw great possibilities in the manufacture of glue, but knew nothing about the actual process, nor did I. We built up a factory and for about a year and a half they stayed in business with me. They took advantage of my ignorance and softness and unloaded their holdings on me and for another four years I struggled desperately to make it a success. The factory itself was equipped to take advantage of every detail of the business. Congress had passed a bill to resume special payment and accepted gold as a standard of values, thereby deflating the paper currency. This of course affected all business and hit me very hard. Glue that formerly had been selling at twenty cents a pound was now offered at four, five, six cents. It could not be produced without a severe loss. This brought on the depression, which caused so many bankruptcies in the country. I avoided a bankruptcy, but gave up the business. After giving up the glue business, I went into the sausage business for a year. That was also unsuccessful and upon receiving an offer to take charge of a fertilizing business in Omaha, I accepted and we moved out there.

After three years in the fertilizing business, I took my savings and on a shoestring started in my own business of butcher supplies and cheese. Prospered slowly. One of S. Birkenwald's and Co.'s salesmen came to Omaha and took half interest in the business, C. B. Liver, by name, 1888. Continued the partnership for ten years and then sold out to him and came back to Milwaukee. Came back just because I was homesick for Milwaukee. In my experience all people who have been born in Wisconsin always seem to come back. Coming back to Milwaukee, I had a position with Weisel & Co. as sales manager, which I retained for twenty-nine years.

AZRIEL KANTER'S JOURNALS, 1890–1899

Azriel Kanter left the town of Ferni in 1892 to eventually settle in Green Bay. As one of the first Russian Jewish immigrants in Green Bay, Kanter became a spiritual leader and founder of the first Jewish congregation, Cnesses Israel. Kanter's journals, begin-ning in 1883 in the community of Lelle, detail what his life had been like in czarist Russia before emigrating. He laments that he had to move from town to town but was never able to eke out a living as a shochet. *He often went without shoes on his feet and lacked money to adequately feed his family. However, it wasn't until the early 1890s that he began to fear for his family's existence as pious Jews living in an increasingly anti-Semitic environment. He tells of his agonizing decision to leave the country, his arduous journey to America, and his newfound sense of self-respect that living in Wisconsin afforded him for the first time in his life. The following are excerpts from Azriel Kanter's journal from the Wisconsin Historical Society archives. They have been translated from the original Yiddish.*

Lelle, September 18, 1890—From Ferni there were twenty families who left for America. Police guards were on duty at the boat. When a non-Jew came aboard, there was no problem; the man could be a thief or a murderer. But when a Jew started to walk up the gangplank—he might be a man of unquestionable honesty and integrity, without the slightest taint—the police will find reasons not to let him go.

Lelle, December 9, 1890—In addition to the poor economic condition, it begins to look as if there is the anti-Semitic factor, too; there are indica-tions that are disturbing. Isaac Leib Blaustein was in Valdav and they sent him threatening messages; one of the tailors there also got one. And a third Jew was simply advised to leave without threats. Leizer and Motte are also in a risky area. I had arranged with Motte to go there to do some slaughtering. He was to pay three rubles per trip since I was to earn nothing [in Ferni] that would have been good, too. But now I'm afraid to go there.

Lelle, January 29, 1891—No doubt it is God's will, but for the moment, at least, situation is worsening. The constable has already put me through a whole interrogation. What do I do, and when do I do it, and where, and how long have I lived here, and are all my papers in order, and so on.

My Cikele [young daughter] asked a question that I believe would be hard to answer even for an adult with a sharp mind. "Mama," she asked, "why would they want to drive us out?" Because we are Jews, said her mother. And Cele says, "But we are good honest Jews!"

Lelle, June 25, 1891—In Corfu they revived the heinous blood-accusa-tion, as a pretext for killing thirteen men and torturing many more until they "confessed." Their property was reduced to ashes and rubble. They were surrounded and imprisoned in their own homes, then driven out to the last one.

Lelle, August 5, 1891—Yesterday I had a letter from Zelmanowitz [good friend] in which he strongly urges me to leave. He does not believe there is much hope that conditions for Jews will get better in Russia. At Court, he says, the priests keep up the "murderers of Christ" theme; therefore, no Jew can be allowed in a Christian house. And the Christians who trade with a Jew must be excommunicated. So, of course, we must leave Russia.

Lelle, October 10, 1891—No question about it, we must escape. But then there is still the question of where to. Where is the Jew liked, or at least tol-erated?

Ferni, November 27, 1891—Now, what do we do? Now, where do we go? I feel like a lost sheep now. I have sold everything and came to Ferni with 150 rubles. It is already nine days that I've been here, and I thank and praise the Almighty that those days are behind me.

Kanter waited in Ferni with his wife and family for five months in constant fear that they would be stopped from leaving for America. He had lost his identification papers and needed to secure a false identity. Finally, after much red tape, his papers were approved and he was allowed to leave for Thomas, West Virginia, where he heard there was a job.

Thomas, West Virginia, April 26, 1892—Long live America! Long live America! Down with Russia! My duty would be to give a thorough account of my situation and a complete description of my journey. But is this really possible? For six weeks I lay cowering in Ferni behind locked doors, in danger every minute. . . . Since childhood I have been in a state of perpetual anxiety about my identification papers.

Virtually the whole town came to see us off. The tears that were shed at our leaving were enough to fill a small river. Half the people of Ferni drove the nine versts [miles] to escort us; we had a horse and carriage. . . . Many inns refused to take us in. Several times the carriage overturned. Our one wish was to live long enough to get to Riga; then we could worry about the rest of the journey. Finally, after four harrowing days of driving, thank and praise Heaven, we pulled into Riga.

At our departure there was again a scene of wailing and weeping and enough tears to form a small lake. It's a shattering experience to separate children from parents—perhaps for good parents from children, sisters from brothers, and so on. My father fell on our necks, imploring us to remain good Jews, not to bring disgrace on him.

Another trip with tiny tots in wintertime, and without a carriage. In Pekkelin I received a certificate under the name of Yossel Itzik Howorwitz, and that is the name I took. The certificate says Jossel Itsik Horowitz is authorized to go to Germany for two weeks (that's me) and still I need a police permit. The anxiety, the fear stays with us. Accursed and damned be the Russian scoundrels who concocted this plan. They drive the Jews out and then don't let them leave.

We were overjoyed at being out of Russia, not quaking at every sound, afraid of every fly. It was like being in the dark and then coming into broad daylight. How bright everything looked! But then, in one instant, our mood changed to despair. We hear that the Committee was resolute in its stand of no more exit permits.

Eventually, the Kanter family (using the alias Horowitz) was given permission to go to Berlin by train, where they boarded the ship headed for America.

Now we had to get the baggage and the children into the railroad car. We climb in and the scene is one of utter pandemonium. There is a terrible crush; people pushing and jostling, scrambling madly with bags and baggage to get the best seats. Women are screaming, children wailing, and the air is full of shouts and curses. We learn quickly there is not water in the car.

[Once in Berlin] we were taken into a house where we waited a long time until everybody was paraded before a doctor to whom we showed our tongues. Then we scrambled into small boats to be ferried quickly to the big one, prophetically named the SS California. The date was February, 1882. We had been among the first to go aboard and a sailor advised us to take lower berths.

The following day it began: bad weather, choppy seas, rocking and swaying, nausea, seasickness, oh, was that awful! What a dreadful thing to see and hear hundreds of grown men and women groaning and moaning and throwing up.

Eight days I lay in my bunk unseen by anyone, face covered, not even undressed. All of our supplies were piled in the bed too and we lay clustered together like mummies. Once we were so shaken up by the ship's tossing, we wound up with our feet sticking straight up in the air, so that we had to hold on with all our might not to fall out of bed. The children, terrified, came up closer and we all huddled together. . . .

On Thursday, *California* weighed anchor in New York Harbor! Everybody was overjoyed. Tomorrow we were entering New York City! Hardly anyone slept that night. Everybody got busy with preparations for the landing. We scrubbed and washed and unpacked our best clothes in honor of the Golden Land. In our excitement there was still room for a bit of worry too. Would we get through Castle Garden [the immigration entry point before Ellis Island was developed] all right? Or would they find problems?

After thirty-one days of hunger, sickness, fear, worry, cold, and dirt, we were taken off the island March 20 [1892]. The small boat was so crowded that our guts were squeezed right out of us. But we got to Castle Rock all right. We had been given baggage checks, and now they only asked names, destinations, and how much money we had and let us go. A few older people who didn't look well were held back for medical examination. Then the rest of us got in a small boat again and headed for New York.

The first years in the Golden Land proved to be difficult ones for the Kanter family. After trying unsuccessfully to eke out a living in Thomas, West Virginia; Parsons, West Virginia; and Chicago, word came from Green Bay, Wisconsin, that they needed a shochet. Reluctantly, Kanter moved his family once again.

Green Bay, October 26, 1894—Thank Heaven, we're already beginning to reckon with the year 5655 [on the Hebrew calendar]. I am very pleased that 5654 is finally gone; it gave me a real bad time. Now there appears to be some reason to hope. I am making a modest living in peace, and slowly begin to pay back my creditors. Right at this point, my debts total just about fifty-five dollars, and I have about forty dollars coming in to me from customers, which I need to collect.

Now, thank Heaven, the atmosphere here is very pleasant. They were extremely pleased at the way I conducted High Holiday services, and there was a minyan [ten men needed for religious prayer] every day throughout the entire week of Succoth [a holiday celebrating the harvest following Yom Kippur].

Green Bay, September 6, 1897—I no longer carry baskets [as a meat peddler]. Now I stay in a butcher shop. I've been getting 5.75 dollars a week as wages and 6 dollars commission.

Green Bay, May 7, 1899—Odd, how irregularly I write from Green Bay. Twenty months now since I've written anything. Can it be because my journal is basically a book of tears, where only laments find welcome, and here this entire period has been the most fruitful and rewarding of my time in America? No, that is not the reason. The real reason is simply that I have been too busy, and haven't had the time; and I thank God for that!

MARTIN DEUTSCHKRON'S ORAL HISTORY

Martin Deutschkron and his wife, Eva, escaped Nazi capture after Kristallnacht, after which they ended up in Wisconsin. Deutschkron related his experiences to a Wisconsin audience in about 1950.

I am a tailor and not a public speaker. As a matter of fact, this is the first time in my life, as you will soon find out.

I was born in Germany as a child of Jewish parents. When Hitler came to power in 1933, I had completed my training as a tailor and was working in my field. In November of 1938 the Nazi storm troopers went on a rampage of destroying Jewish homes and business establishments. I was working at the time in Berlin, Kurfverrstem Dam, a fashionable business district, as a custom tailor in a shop, which was located on the second floor. That afternoon a group of storm troopers forcibly entered the shop, shouting, "All Jews get out!" When people did not comply fast enough the troopers kicked us and pushed us down the stairs, headfirst. At the foot of the stairs additional storm troopers were lined up, hitting us with sticks as we were trying to escape. This night is being referred to as the "crystal night" because of the large-scale breaking of windows, chandeliers, furniture, and anything breakable.

Following the "crystal night" many Jews were put into concentration camps. We also were required to identify ourselves by wearing a Star of David on all our outside clothing. Also, Jews were drafted to do forced labor in factories manufacturing war equipment. We were working in separate detachments under prisonlike conditions. Those who lived less than seven kilometers from the factory were not allowed to use any transportation. Those who lived farther away could use public transportation to get to work, but for no other purpose. Working hours were ten to twelve hours a day. We could walk on the premises only in groups and under guard. Pay was considerably lower than what was paid to others. No one was allowed to quit.

At first only Jews not engaged in war production were gathered and shipped east to concentration camps. Eventually even those who were working in factories producing war materials were taken to concentration camps. On October 28, 1942, the Gestapo came to pick up my parents, my wife's parents, and her fifteen-year-old sister and took them to a gathering place for deportation to a concentration camp. My wife's parents were sent back to their apartment to continue their work of repairing uniforms, while my wife's fifteen-year-old sister had to remain there. Neither she nor my parents were ever heard of again. In spite of our many efforts after the war to learn of their fate, not even a trace could ever be found. It is suspected that this whole transport of eight hundred to nine hundred people were destroyed immediately before reaching any destination. The rest of our family, along with others, were at different times taken to concentration camps where they perished of hard labor or the majority fed to the gas ovens.

In January of 1943, the Gestapo came to arrest us while we were not home. When we did get home, the janitor alerted us and we escaped arrest and deportation to a concentration camp.

We then started to live underground. Living underground was living like a fugitive—not being "registered" with the police department, which was and still is required of every German resident and visitor; not having ration cards for food and clothing; and not being able to go to the air raid shelters. Our constant problem was finding a hiding place. Since it was hazardous to stay at one place too long, we could never stay longer than a week at one place—we lived in constant fear, like an animal running from hiding place to hiding place. In the course of two and a half years in hiding we found temporary refuge in such different places as a tailor shop, where during the day we worked and at night slept on an ironing table. We stayed in a farmhouse; in an unheated porch of a cottage; in a basement where we got bombed. For a week we stayed with a family for whom we did janitor work. Some knew our identity, helping us to find place after place. Others did not. In some instances, we were denounced to the Gestapo. The Secret Police was constantly on our trail, but we were lucky enough to elude them.

The only way in which we were able to surface at times was when there was an absolute necessity, with the help of forged personal documents made out under assumed names. The widow of a German soldier who had been killed sold me her husband's passport. Germans who were opposed to Hitler got us in touch with members of the British espionage service, who as part of their work, forged papers for people like us. These papers were absolute lifesavers because in Europe in general and in

Germany in particular, even today one can be stopped at any time to prove his identity. I cannot even begin to give you an idea of what it was like to live in constant fear of being caught for two and a half years. It would have meant immediate death. At all times I carried on me a gun and a small hand grenade for the purpose of killing myself and my wife in case we were caught. The fate waiting for us would have been much worse. Fortunately, the war came to an end on May 5, 1945, and with it the liberation of the world from Nazi tyranny.

SELECTED BIBLIOGRAPHY

Brawarsky, Sandee, and Deborah Mark. *Two Jews, Three Opinions: A Collection of Twentieth-Century American Jewish Quotes.* New York: Perigree Books, 1998.

Dimont, Max I. *Jews, God and History.* 2nd ed. New York: Mentor, 1994.

The Golden History of Beth Israel Center 1949–1999. Madison, WI: Temple Beth Israel Center, 1999.

Gurda, John. *One People, Many Paths: A History of Jewish Milwaukee.* Milwaukee, WI: Jewish Museum Milwaukee, 2009.

Laxova, Renata. *Letter to Alexander.* Cincinnati, OH: Custom Editorial Productions, 2001.

Matzner, Robert. *Prisoner 19053: A True Story of a Fourteen Year Old Boy Who Spent Three Years in a Nazi Concentration Camp.* Sheboygan Falls, WI: Sheboygan County Historical Research Center, 2008.

Moses Montefiore Synagogue 50th Anniversary Book. Appleton, WI: Moses Montefiore Congregation, 1972.

Muchin, Andrew. *Chosen Towns: The Story of Jews in Wisconsin's Small Communities.* DVD. Documentary produced by University of Wisconsin–Milwaukee and the Wisconsin Society for Jewish Learning's Wisconsin Small Jewish Communities History Project, 2008.

Nesbit, Robert C., and William F. Thomas. *Wisconsin: A History.* 2nd ed. Madison: University of Wisconsin Press, 2004.

Rathburn, Arthur, and Ursula Rathburn. *No More Tears Left Behind: The Remarkable Life Story of Holocaust Survivor Eva Deutschkron.* Dane, WI: Fort Dane Books, 2009.

Sachar, Howard M. *A History of the Jews in America.* New York: Vintage Books, 1993.

Seiler, Mark R. *Jewish Community of Stevens Point.* Stevens Point, WI: Portage County Historical Society, 2008.

Sidran, Ben. *There Was a Fire: Jews, Music, and the American Dream.* 2nd ed. London: Nardis Books, an imprint of Unlimited Media, Ltd., 2012.

Spalding, Henry D. *Encyclopedia of Jewish Humor: From the Biblical Times to the Modern Age.* New York: Jonathan David, 1979.

Stevens, Michael E., ed. *Remembering the Holocaust.* Madison, WI: State Historical Society of Wisconsin, 1997.

Swarsensky, Manfred. *From Generation to Generation: The Story of the Madison Jewish Community.* Madison, WI: American Printing Company, 1955.

Swarsensky, Manfred. *Intimates and Ultimates.* Madison, WI: Edgewood College, 1981.

Swichkow, Louis J., and Lloyd P. Gardner. *History of Jews in Milwaukee.* Philadelphia: Jewish Publication Society of America, 1963.

We Were There, World War II: The Milwaukee Jewish Experience. Milwaukee, WI: Milwaukee Jewish Archives, 1996.

ACKNOWLEDGMENTS

This story could not be told without the people who lived it. My deep gratitude goes out to Wisconsin residents Albert Beder, who survived the Dachau concentration camp; Renata Laxova, who was rescued from Nazi occupation of her home in the Czech Republic; and Waclaw Szybalski, who as a member of the Catholic faith put his own life at risk to rescue his Polish Jewish neighbors. The life experiences that they related to me provide a glimpse at the factors that made it possible for Jewish survivors of the Holocaust to live freely and productively in Wisconsin.

Thanks, too, to Harold Holman, who has been a member of the Sheboygan Jewish community since birth and has done much to help it survive; to Dr. Jay Larkey, who, remembering a time of discrimination against Jews, fought for the rights of the African American community in Milwaukee during the 1960s; to Sam Moss and Sam Onheiber, who shared stories of their happy experiences in the Greenbush neighborhood of Madison; to Ghita Bessman, who recounted her husband Leonard's heroic deeds in World War II; to Sylvia Grunes, who recalled her childhood experiences in the Arbeiter Ring; to rabbis Simcha Prombaum in La Crosse and Dena Feingold of Kenosha, who spoke of their Jewish experiences in small-town Wisconsin; to Leonard Smuglin and Julia Kirchevsky, both of whom recalled their respective experiences of leaving the Soviet Union in the latter 1900s to lead a freer existence in Wisconsin; and to Paul Soglin and Ed Feige, who recounted their memories of the turbulent war protests on the University of Wisconsin campus and the participation of the state's residents in the civil rights movement of the south. Each has added a valuable perspective on Jewish life in Wisconsin's small towns and larger cities.

My gratitude goes out to the earlier settlers, people who are no longer living but who have left their legacy in the form of photos, letters, and journals. Their foresight in leaving such historical treasures is a gift to future generations who can take pride in the efforts and courage of their forebears.

The help I received in accessing such valuable materials made my research of the vast information much easier. For this I particularly want to thank Jay Hyland, archivist at the Jewish Museum in Milwaukee. My appreciation also goes to Joel Alpert, who provided photos that reflect the thriving Jewish community of Sheboygan's past; Phyllis Garelick, who had a hand in recording the history of the Jewish life in Appleton; Phyllis Weisbard, who skillfully organized photos of Madison's yesteryear; and Dina Weinebach, who made them accessible to me at the Jewish Federation of Madison.

Historians Jonathan Pollack, faculty member of Madison College, and Tim Crain, who taught at the Center for Jewish Studies at the University of Wisconsin in Madison and Milwaukee, were invaluable resources and fact-checkers for me in my quest for historical accuracy. I thank them both for the time and effort they offered in reading my manuscript.

I also received valuable input from rabbis Laurie Zimmerman, Jonathan Baitch, Joshua Ben-Gideon, and Andrea Steinberger regarding the various practices and concepts of the Jewish faith. I am grateful for their guidance.

To all who helped the story of Jews in Wisconsin become a published book, I offer my gratitude, with special thanks to Erika Wittekind, who carefully reviewed and edited my manuscript at the Wisconsin Historical Society Press.

In addition, I want to thank my husband, Marc Cohen, who enthusiastically offered his support for this project. His father, who left the turbulence of Russia, arrived in Fond du Lac in 1921 as a fruit peddler and eventually built a successful produce business in the Fox Valley area of the state. Born and raised in Appleton, Marc has lived part of this story firsthand. He and all but one of his three siblings continue to live in Wisconsin, the state that has offered them so very much.

And last, but certainly not least, to my own ancestors who wisely and courageously left their countries of origin in Russia and Poland to pave the way for a free life in America. As a recipient of their bravery, I am forever thankful.

THE AUTHOR

Sheila Terman Cohen has written three Badger Biography books for the Wisconsin Historical Society Press: *Mai Ya's Long Journey*, *Gaylord Nelson: Champion for Our Earth*, and *Sterling North and the Story of Rascal*. *Mai Ya's Long Journey* received first-place recognition by both the Council of Wisconsin Writers and the Midwest Independent Publishers Association and was listed in the University of Wisconsin's Cooperative Children's Book Center's publication, *Choices*. The national book award group, Next Generation, named *Gaylord Nelson: Champion for Our Earth* the first-place winner in children's juvenile nonfiction literature. As a freelance writer, Cohen has also written articles that have been published in a variety of newspapers, including the *Wisconsin State Journal*, the *Capital Times*, *La Comunidad*, and *Isthmus*.

Before studying journalism at the University of Wisconsin, Cohen taught English as a Second Language in the Madison schools. She and her husband have been longtime residents of Madison, Wisconsin, where they raised their family.

INDEX